A Path Not Chosen

Walking in a Cancer World

Carolyn A. Rhodes

2020

First published 2024

Copyright © Carolyn A. Rhodes 2020

Additional work – copyright © Mark Rhodes 2020, 2021, 2022 and 2023

All rights reserved. No part of this publication may be reproduced, stored in a retrieval system, or transmitted, in any form, or by any means (electronic, mechanical, photocopying, recording or otherwise) without the prior written permission of the author's legal representative(s).

The author's legal representatives have no control over, nor any responsibility howsoever arising in connection with, anything written in or presented in this book.

All photographs taken by the authors.

This book is sold subject to the condition that it shall not, by way of trade or otherwise, be lent, hired out, or otherwise circulated in any form of binding or cover without the author's or author's legal representatives' prior written consent other than that which is published, and without a similar condition including this condition being imposed on the subsequent purchaser.

Visit www.apathnotchosen.com to discover more.

CAROLYN RHODES was a devoted wife and mother who discovered her academic career later in life, following an earlier passion for books. After having a family, she gained an MBA. Her career culminated as Head of Department of the new Study Advice Service at The University of Hull, which facilitated the progression of 'A' level students into tertiary education at the university. It was her passion. While at Hull University, she gained a Doctorate in Education and became a Fellow of the Royal Society of Arts, Manufactures & Commerce. After retiring, Carolyn was asked to join the board of governors at the leading local independent school. But Carolyn was more than just her career. Labradors were always part of her life, as were daffodils, for ever her favourite flower. Her legacy, amongst many, is to share her journey and lessons learnt navigating 'a path not chosen'.

Dedicated to the memory of Carolyn Rhodes

Time passes – Love remains

This is a handbook for living with cancer and becoming stronger than before, for those newly diagnosed with cancer, those struggling to adjust, and for those carers or professionals looking to learn from personal experience. Each part can be read independently, or in any order.

Accept what is, let go of what was, and have faith in what will be.

A Time to Just . . . Be

By the same author

Don't Stop Me Now: The Personal Journey of a Middle-Aged Odyssey to the Caribbean

PART I: MY FIRST STEPS ON THE PATH NOT CHOSEN

Part 1:	**My first steps on the path not chosen**	**Page**
1.1	Life and context	12
1.2.	Initial diagnosis and treatment	18
1.3.	Devastation and fear	27
1.4.	Surgery and beyond	33

Part 2.	**Challenges: negotiating the minefield**	
2.1.	Chemo, scans and other tests	40
2.2.	Feelings and emotions	44
2.2.1	Isolation	44
2.2.2	Emotional health	45
2.2.3	Processing the diagnosis	47
2.2.4	Acceptance	48
2.2.5	Reflection	49
2.3.	Planning and reprioritisation	51
2.3.1	Having a strategy	51
2.3.2	Diet	55
2.3.3	Trust	57
2.3.4	Recurrence	59

Part 3.	**A creative strategy**	
3.1.	Practical: support the body's healing through nutrition and exercise	76
3.2	Emotional: decrease stress, particularly emotional stress, and have a trusted support team	79
3.3	Behavioural: count blessings, give life meaning, and a new purpose. Create a new normal.	80
3.4	Spiritual: beliefs, religion, meditation	83

	Bonus benefit	86
Part 4:	**Conclusion**	
4.1	Acknowledgement and acceptance is the hardest part of all	90
4.2	Be creative and resilient	90
4.3	The cancer path is personal	91
4.4	Developing medical students' understanding	92
Part 5:	**A final word and message**	96
Part 6:	**Involving other people**	
6.1	A note from a friend	102
6.2	A note from a minister	104
6.3	A son's perspective	105
6.3.1	Approach	105
6.3.2	Context	105
6.3.3	From the beginning	107
6.3.4	Oncologist appointments	111
6.3.5	Other things you can do	117
6.3.6	The hospice	122
6.3.7	Darkness	125
6.3.8	After the darkness – practical steps	125
6.3.9	The funeral	128
6.3.10	After the funeral	129
6.3.11	Do not forget about you	133
Annex – Some cancer organisations and their contact details		136
Index		141

PART 1:

My first steps on the path not chosen

Part 1: My first steps on the path not chosen

1.1 Life and context

This is the story of one person's battle to survive trauma, and create, amid the chaos, some normality: a new, totally different normality, evolving from the challenging rollercoaster of events. It is a personal story of shock, intense fear, pain and a deep pit of blackness. That person is me.

It is also a story of incredible kindness, outstanding patience, and amazing support – both practical and psychological. It involves the exceptional medical expertise and dedication of a variety of National Health Service (NHS) professionals. Whoever coined the phrase 'You don't know how strong you are until you have no other option' was not being flippant: they were speaking from experience. I learnt this through experience too.

Who am I? Well, no world leader for sure, nor even a minor celebrity. And, heaven forbid, no 'wannabe' or media junkie. Just an ordinary woman who is a wife, mother, sister and friend to those who inhabit her small world. That is me. I am lucky to have a husband to whom I have been married for over 50 years (I was a very young bride!) and am blessed with two adult sons, who are possibly my greatest achievement and contribution to the wider world. The world in which I lived, worked and played was secure and comfortable.

Brought up in a loving family, privately educated at great cost to average, middle-class parents, I was destined to have a reasonably comfortable life. For sure, I had to work hard, be a well-behaved and responsible young woman, and contribute to society through care for others. Putting others first and treating everyone with kindness were key attributes that were fundamental elements in my life. I know I have been very lucky to have had such a stable upbringing, one that was to provide a bedrock on which my subsequent reactions to my journey with cancer were based.

After marrying early and focussing entirely on managing the home and bringing up a family (not always the easiest of options), I gradually undertook various training courses as the children got older. The boys were using computers at school and from time to time they would have a problem that needed solving. At the time the most technical thing I had used was the vacuum cleaner; so, clearly, I needed to upgrade my skills and learned to use a computer at a basic level. I also volunteered at the local hospice, and after spending some time working in the Bereavement Support Office, I moved to the In-Patient Unit. The very first volunteer training session I attended was entitled 'Why me?' The answer, I recall, was a firm 'Why not me?' It was a lesson that would come back to haunt me years later.

I found the work challenging but interesting, and loved being needed and valued. Caring for other people was one of my core values, and this was what I could contribute to the world around me. Perhaps I also subconsciously hoped that, by putting in effort now, I would earn enough Brownie points to buy me a cancer-free future. I even studied for a Diploma in Counselling and Therapy, writing a dissertation on Counselling in a Hospice Setting. How ironic. This seems uncannily prophetic in the light of what was to come; namely, two primary cancers and a total nightmare of shock, pain and fear.

But let's move hastily on. One training course followed another, covering a variety of technological and management-related subjects. These ranged from eventually qualifying as a Licentiate of the Chartered Institute of Personnel and Development, through to becoming a Fellow of the Royal Society of Arts. I also found time to complete a Certificate in Landscape and Horticultural Design, solely to meet my increasing passion for the land and gardening! I landed a job managing a research project at the regional university's local college, and this was all the springboard I needed to establish an ongoing, structured discipline for my own learning and development – my chosen path.

Through several twists and turns, my career in Higher Education took off and I soared through the ranks, much to everyone's surprise, especially my own. When I retired, I was Head of the University's Academic Skills Development Service, I had two degrees, as well as a specialist MBA, and had recently completed a Doctorate in Educational Policy. The latter study was intensely focussed on the psychological needs of the adult learner, a difficult subject if ever there was one. Not a bad record for a late starter. But I do like a challenge ...

I retired relatively early and took on new challenges, becoming a governor of a local independent fee-paying school my sons had attended some years previously. I also became a member of the board of the hospice, the same hospice that I had volunteered in so many years earlier; which gave me a 'both sides of the coin' viewpoint. Yet again, it was satisfying to be able to give something back to such a worthwhile community.

For several intense years I had worked away from home. I had bought a small cottage in a nearby market town in which to live during the week, so I had effectively been running two separate households, and there had been little time to spare for personal interests. After my retirement, my hobbies resurfaced; I now attacked the garden with renewed enthusiasm, and spent many happy hours walking our two Labradors in the countryside. My husband and I made a couple of exciting trips to the Caribbean, sailing with friends on a chartered catamaran and learning the fine maritime skills involved in mixing rum cocktails!

We travelled a lot and were lucky to visit some 'once in a lifetime' places such as Australia, Russia, China and Alaska, but we most regularly visited Scotland, a place with which we both feel an affinity. It was on one of our return journeys after a delightful holiday on the Black Isle, north of Inverness, that I recall saying to my husband, David, that I felt better than I had for years. Relaxed, energised, and content. But sadly, it was not to last.

Key points

- While there may be difficult times ahead, there will also be kindness.

- It may seem there is no rhyme nor reason as to why you have cancer, but always remember: you are stronger than you think you are.

1.2 Initial diagnosis and treatment

We returned from Scotland at the end of September 2014, to a mountain of mail – the usual mix of bills and charity letters, and occasional surprises. One of my surprises was a recall from a mammogram that I had had before we went to Scotland a couple of weeks earlier. During the following few days, friends reassured me that 'everyone' has a recall, and I was positively unusual in not having had one before, so David and I went along to the appointment without too much anxiety. Indeed, after the usual tests and biopsy, I was told by the clinician quite casually that it was unlikely anything would be found, and that, even if something were to be found, the chances were that it would be benign.

Within two days we had gone off to London to stay with son no. 2, Mark, and were not unduly perturbed. The main cause of anxiety that weekend was being taken to the top of the Shard! I dislike heights or lifts, although the fortifying power of a G & T helped considerably. This combination certainly cleared my mind of other risks that, at worst, were considered minimal and, at best, non-existent.

The following Tuesday we went back and presented ourselves to the Breast Cancer Centre at the region's main hospital. The clinician, the same one I had seen the previous week, told me quite plainly, 'Yes, there was a cancerous tumour, and, by the way, you will be having surgery two weeks today. Do you want a lumpectomy or mastectomy?' This was to be the start of my personal relationship with cancer – a path not chosen.

'Stunned' just does not do justice to our joint reaction. It was surreal: my normality seemed to have been stripped away, exposing a raw, deep, black new world. I wanted to press 'rewind' and start the conversation again, but it was clear this lady had a busy schedule and an urgent need for an intelligible response from me. I struggled to make any response at all. All I could think of was that, on the day when they had scheduled my surgery, I was also due to be on an interview panel for a new head teacher for the independent school of which I was a governor and education consultant. My unthinking reaction was to say that I had a commitment that day. That was just the first of many clashes and conflicts I would face between my previous normality and my new reality; my response did not go down at all well.

Then the new reality suddenly hit me hard: 'Cancer! I have cancer. No, it cannot be true! Why me? What have I ever done?!' First there was pure fear, after which, uncontrollable panic set in, and my stress levels soared, fuelled by both dread and terror. Poor David had gone ashen and was stunned into silence, not something he is well known for. I found myself agreeing to a lumpectomy, and we left the Centre, heading straight for the Costa Coffee shop in the main hospital, to gather our frenzied thoughts and process the horrific news.

It was at this stage that my previously unassailable trust in the medics wavered. How could a doctor be almost cavalier about saying that the worst outcome could be a benign tumour; then switch direction with little preamble to saying it was something serious enough to warrant almost immediate surgery?

By the time we returned to our parked car, the immediate shock had turned into floods of tears. The reality had kicked in and I could not stop shaking, and sobbed uncontrollably. I rang my sister Susan, but was so incoherent that David took over the call to convey the news. Our sons, Andrew and Mark, were shocked but rallied with support as best they could. The surprise came from the reactions of close friends, which ranged from stunned silence to a hearty exhortation to 'just think positive'. The next few days brought more tears and varied reactions from others, as I struggled to come to terms with what seemed a death sentence. Tumour, cancer, death, seemed the natural progression in my mind, and I continued to shake with anxiety and undiluted fear as the day of the surgery drew ever closer.

At no stage during the following days did anyone from the clinic ring to see if I was calmer or had any questions following the meeting's outcome. Professional advice or signposts to help would have been useful. A panicked brain does not always think logically, so ringing a support organisation such as Macmillan did not come immediately to mind.

I must note here that the support from my immediate family was simply amazing. One devoted husband, my two attentive sons – who until then had been completely ignorant of female cancers – and my sister and brother-in-law, to whom I am very close, had all provided a steady hand to hold. Specific close friends, including one living many miles distant, gave unstinting support even though the telephone calls were often perilously waterlogged with tears.

Now, on the positive side, this timeframe was showcasing the NHS at its best, but to me, grappling with my own perception of the word 'cancer' and what that meant for me, everything seemed to be moving far too fast; it took some time to digest what was happening. Whichever way you look at it, being diagnosed with cancer can have a devastating and frightening effect, although a lot does depend on the type and stage of the tumour, and the individual's understanding and personal reaction. Suddenly, the fragility of life becomes starkly apparent, as well as our total lack of control over our health. It does not matter if you have been a good human being, or have lots of money or a big house, or important contacts. None of that can make any difference to the outcome. Without good health, you have nothing.

On the scheduled date, I went in for my operation, a quivering nervous wreck. A kind Macmillan nurse, seeing and hearing how upset I was, accompanied me to the theatre, probably more to keep me from running away and streaking back down the corridor.

The surgery went well and I returned home the following day, a little shaky but pleased that the worst was over. As expected, there was considerable soreness, and some simple practical advice on coping with it would have helped. Apart from instructions not to lift a heavy teapot, very little else had been forthcoming. It would have helped enormously to be told to wear a loose-fitting crop top in place of a bra for a week or two. Very few of us keep a bra two sizes too big in our lingerie drawer, which would have helped to accommodate the significant and sore chest swelling.

But not a whisper had been said about this. I felt battered and bruised, but otherwise over the worst. I followed all the post-surgery instructions to the letter and started the physio exercises to help regain some flexibility. On discharge from hospital, I was given a leaflet outlining certain exercises to do at home at a given stage in the weeks of recovery. This, at least, was a useful guide.

At the post-surgery meeting I was told about the treatment plan. I was worried I would need chemotherapy, and, when they mentioned it, I was terrified. The nightmare of chemo was threatening to enter my life, bringing with it a dark cloud of uncertainty. But I was one of the lucky ones because I drew the radiotherapy straw. This would mean five weeks of daily trips to the nearest cancer treatment hospital, taking me up to, and over, Christmas and New Year. A merry prospect indeed.

Feeling debilitated from the anxiety and stress, not to mention the actual surgery and anaesthetic, I started the radiotherapy programme the following week. First, I had an appointment with the Nuclear Medicine Department, not to be rocketed into space, but to be the recipient of a tattoo to 'mark the spot' for the radiotherapy beam. There followed five long, hard, tiring weeks of driving 110 miles every day to receive 15 minutes' worth of radiotherapy. We got weekends off (possibly for good behaviour or at least for turning up), but were not allowed to miss treatments on weekdays; even if it was Christmas Eve or New Year's Eve, the appointments were obligatory. It was not an easy time, although the practical support from family and friends was amazing – the lifts family and friends gave us to and from the hospital were of great comfort to me, and allowed for a good chat and gossip session with each 'taxi driver'. It is amazing how much you can catch up on during a 110-mile journey.

I was due to finish the course in the third week of January, and the closer the end came, the more tired and emotional I became. In fact, on the day I finished the treatment, I was in tears more than once. I had expected I would be delirious with happiness at having completed the course, but that was not to be, as I struggled to accept that my treatment for breast cancer was actually over. I was tired, sore, and struggling to be me again. It was like being pushed over a cliff edge, with no safety net of regular medical meetings to support my fragile state. It felt as if I had been spat out at the end of a many-staged process, hit a brick wall and then found myself drifting through an oppressive dark emptiness. A weird and isolating experience. By this time, I had been assigned a Macmillan breast cancer nurse. But, as in most hospitals, she had limited hours and a huge list of patients in her workload so it was not easy to access support and reassurance at the point of need.

I finished radiotherapy on a Thursday, and five days later, the following Tuesday, I visited my general practitioner (GP) for advice on some side effects. Little did I know that the nightmare had only just begun, and I was nowhere near experiencing the horrors that were yet to come. It truly is a blessing that we do not know what lies ahead: our ignorance means we go on blundering through life and just have to cope as best we can. No one would take the path I was on out of choice.

The human spirit is an amazing thing, carrying one through unimaginable difficulties in life, cancer included. It is not a question of 'being positive', helpful though that may be; it is a matter of trust, faith and determination to hang on to life against some pretty grim odds. And that leads me nicely on to the next hurdle. But first . . .

Key points

- Cancer can affect anyone, irrespective of background, diet, personality, gender or ethnicity.

- Diagnosis can bring shock, panic and fear – all normal reactions.

- Friends and family may react in diverse ways, and not always as you might expect. Each person can process what is going on differently.

- If facing surgery, ask for practical advice from the medical team as well as emotional support.
- Be kind to yourself, be patient, and allow yourself time to adjust to new situations and procedures.
- Ask for help if you are feeling isolated; that is what the medical team should be there for.
- Remember, you are stronger than you think.

1.3 Devastation and fear

On that Tuesday, after examining me, the GP suggested I go to the local hospital for a scan. He suspected I had bladder retention, although qualified this by saying it was usually men who suffered from it. Not a propitious start. At Accident & Emergency (A&E), they confirmed the swelling in my lower abdomen was fluid retention from the bladder and, despite my repeated insistence that I had already emptied my bladder, they fitted me with a catheter. Not the easiest or most comfortable procedure and it required skill in walking with it strapped to my leg. It also required the wearing of wide-leg trousers during the day, and a Heath Robinson contraption utilising a coat hanger on the side of the bed on which to hang the bag at night. It was a learning curve like no other.

After three days it was clear the catheter was having no effect whatsoever on the swelling, so I returned to the GP for advice. He seemed nonplussed, but suggested I stay with it until the week was up as the catheter was due to be removed the following Tuesday. After the offending article had been removed and it was apparent that the problem was still there, I was sent for an ultrasound scan, which prompted a discussion in A&E as to whether I needed to be referred to a urologist or a gynaecologist. They decided on the latter course, and

I met with a pleasant gynaecologist who explained that the scan 'had shown something suspicious'. This was to prove the major understatement of the year. I was to be admitted while they decided what to do, which, in my highly sensitised state post-radiotherapy, was not reassuring.

Then, shortly after I arrived on a large open ward later that day, the next trauma unfolded. I was lying in bed rather upset and frightened about the turn of events, where my body no longer seemed to belong to me. Two young female doctors, probably not yet 30 years old, approached my bed and closed the curtains around us. They went to either side of the bed and took hold of my left and right hand. One even knelt beside the bed. I was horrified! What was happening? What did they know? They just kept saying, 'We're so sorry.' I was hysterical. It was as though I had been given a death sentence, and I might not last the week.

Do medical students not get any training on how to deal with such delicate, frightening situations? They were certainly demonstrating care and sympathy, but careful consideration is needed when it comes to how an already traumatised patient, such as myself, might react when what is needed is calm reassurance. Clearly, they knew what was suspected, but equally clearly had forgotten to tell the patient! I cannot remember if my blood pressure was taken that evening but, if it was, I guess it would have blown the top off the tube. I was distraught and exhausted from the emotional impact and sobbed into my pillow; and, as I continued to cry uncontrollably, the nurses moved me to a small side room so I did not upset the other patients, who were settling down for the night. That night was not one I would ever care to repeat. I could not eat and did not sleep, but just quietly continued to sob through the dark hours of the night, still none the wiser as to my prognosis.

A dear friend texted me at about 7.30 a.m. to see how I was, and, 15 minutes later, appeared on the ward. Despite being told it was an 'unusual visiting time', they reluctantly let her into my room, where I swamped her with more floods of tears. What a true friend, and such sensitive kindness. This special friend has a wonderful calming influence on me (and most people) and she soothed me in her gentle way. We prayed together for the strength and courage to move forward and when she left me to go to work, I was much readier to face whatever the future had in store.

My next visitor was the kind gynaecologist who confirmed that she had referred me to a surgeon, again at the main cancer hospital all those miles away. This was the same hospital at which I had just finished radiotherapy and had hoped I would not see again quite so soon. I left my local hospital that day utterly shell-shocked and in a deep pit of fear and despair.

Trauma and fear on this level have a devastating effect on the body, both physically and psychologically. Your appetite goes, sleep is difficult or disrupted, your heart rate increases or loses its natural, normal rhythm, tears flow unprompted, fear triggers shakiness in the body, and shock makes the body feel weak and exhausted. Tactless comments exhorting one to 'think positive' only increased the stress and pressure, as if all we had to do was to try that bit harder, and suddenly all would be well again. But that isn't how it works. It is a black hole of despair, a deep pit of devastating darkness that closes in and obliterates the light.

So it was that I struggled through the week that followed, before seeing the next consultant surgeon back at the cancer hospital. We were fortunate to have a medical friend accompany us to act as interpreter for any medical jargon or procedures that left us dumbfounded. The news was not good – the diagnosis was that I had ovarian cancer, which is often called 'the silent killer'. I can honestly say that the conversation left me speechless, if only because none of the words that I heard registered in my brain. The surgeon could have been speaking Mandarin for all I understood; the shock had just blown my mind into smithereens, so it was just as well our doctor friend could prune out unnecessary information and simplify the explanations of what they were proposing to do.

A date was set for surgery, before which there were significant warnings of possibly catastrophic side effects. It was stressed that it would be major surgery and termed an 'optimal debulk', which did not sound very glamorous. It meant that, once I was opened up, they would take out anything and everything that looked suspicious. Although the ovaries were the prime target, ovarian cancer was not discussed at any stage. It all sounded hugely frightening and drastic. But it never occurred to me not to go ahead with the surgery. By then, I had complete trust in the team and the decisions they were making, and continued to have this same level of trust in the hospital and the oncologist assigned to me at the time.

There followed a week of unbelievable anxiety, the like of which I had never known before. It was a week of little sleep, palpitations, no appetite, unstoppable tears, and a brain that could not produce a logical or useful thought. It was just plain terrifying, all-consuming fear: fear of major surgery, fear of blood loss, fear of pain, but ultimately a deep, gnawing fear of dying. It was to be a stony path to walk, with many unexpected twists and turns, and the odd storm thrown in for good measure.

Key points

- Be firm about your symptoms. You know your own body better than anyone else does.

- Most medics are kind and want to help: that is why they went into medicine. If anyone upsets you, do not hesitate to let them know so they are aware of it, or refer it on to someone more senior.

- Ask your GP to help with symptoms of anxiety or stress. Talk to the people who will understand you. Ask for help.

- Remember, if the NHS is investing resources in you, for example through surgery and/or treatment, then there are good grounds to hope for a positive outcome.

1.4 Surgery and beyond

It was not a well or happy person who entered the hallowed halls of the cancer hospital the following week. After months of shock, anaesthetics, surgery, radiotherapy, trauma and, finally, intense stress, I presented myself to them and put myself in their hands, safe in the knowledge that this was a highly regarded hospital and the best place to be. My accompanying team, walking either side of me, were my husband David and younger son Mark. They were both stalwarts in the face of adversity, and incredibly fierce in their protection of me. We were due to arrive for 2 p.m., but spent the following three hours in a small room waiting to be admitted. I remember that we spent the time playing I-Spy! The ward was incredibly busy with clusters of small units, and staff and visitors mingling like a medical version of Kings Cross Station.

Eventually I was shown to my own large room, a luxury in an NHS hospital – quite unexpected but very much appreciated. My escort team left to check into their local accommodation for the next couple of days, and I settled in. They had been advised to stay locally for the first couple of days, as I might need intensive care. So they had booked a good guest house in the lovely market town where my second home, and working base had been some years earlier. The night came, but not sleep.

Despite being fairly cloistered in my own room, the noise level was almost deafening. The room was opposite the ward kitchen and the staff room, and the hours of darkness did not stop the metallic clanking of trolleys, shouting of instructions or the banging of metal doors. But a small price to pay for the expertise and care on offer.

With little sleep, and my anxiety levels off the scale, I was not in a good way the following morning. As the operating theatre beckoned, I was assigned a young assistant to sit with me, keep me company and make sure I was as calm as possible. Not an easy task. I cannot remember what we talked about, I guess some very easy inconsequential stuff, but she kept the tears from flowing and stayed with me until my bed was wheeled out through seemingly endless miles of corridors. At all times the staff were friendly and chatty, apparently trying to keep me fully occupied to distract me from becoming more agitated.

The arrivals area in the theatre complex was like a huge underground carpark, but with better lighting and a lot cleaner. Every surface was covered in brilliant white paint, with bright lights everywhere, which was the last thing I remember from that day.

The next few days passed in a blur, not least as I had a bad reaction to the morphine that was being administered to me by drip. There were tubes and monitors around the bed, with pings and plops echoing every so often in the quiet room. Visitors came and went, with my husband and son an ongoing presence whenever I surfaced from my drug-induced stupor. The surgeon, a lovely lady, came to visit too, and we spent time talking about the Black Isle in Scotland, which she also knew well, rather than the massive operation over which she had just presided. Our elder son Andrew, my sister Susan, and her husband John came to visit, but close friends weren't allowed until later, as I slowly recovered from the major surgery.

I returned home in a very fragile state after eight days in hospital. One of the first visitors at home was my GP, who was extremely complimentary about the needlework performed on my lengthy incision. It had taken me some days to bring myself to look at it, but I had to admit that it was pretty neat work despite its horrifying length. Close family, that is, my sons, sister and brother-in-law, were amazing in their support for us, as we struggled to come to terms with everything that had happened. A lot of friends kept a safe distance. I like to think this was to give me peace and space but I suspect that, for a few, it was a terrifying problem that was too close to home. A lot of people just do not know what to do or say after such a devastating diagnosis.

One particular friend just kept repeating 'think positive' as a mantra, as though this magic phrase would swipe my memory bank and everything would go back to normal. Another friend could only say that she knew just how I felt. This was the worst thing for me to hear: it frequently reduced me to rage and tears. No one knows how they will react after a series of terrifying events and diagnoses, but I found it insensitive, presumptive and hurtful, particularly as the person involved had no experience of cancer in their family, thankfully.

My own personal fear and pain felt unacknowledged. I admit I was sensitive to everything, but who would not be after such a traumatic few months? Another friend would appear clutching a casserole or just leave it by the door, showing a true understanding of what help might be valued. One good friend just kept up a series of kind, supportive texts, while another lit a daily candle and prayed that all would be well eventually, which was nice to know.

Such a variety of responses gave me a new perspective. A dear friend offered to drive up just for a hug and to hold my hand for the day, despite the several hundred miles that lay between her home and mine. Kindness knows no bounds. And kindness has the most powerful influence on our well-being. Just knowing that genuine offer was there was enough to stem the tears, and realise that love and kindness do conquer most things. It certainly makes a difference and can totally change the course of a day. Knowing that someone who cares is metaphorically walking beside you is the greatest gift you can give a cancer patient. It was to become an essential factor in the care and support I needed for what came next.

Key points

- Appreciate the small things, that is, loving support, the kindness of strangers, access to medical expertise, and the natural world (such as birdsong, flowers and sunsets).

- Allow plenty of time to recover from surgery, both physically and emotionally. Keep your home environment calm and quiet.

- Protect yourself from insensitive comments and initially keep visitors to a minimum. Do not be pressurised into having visitors you do not want or need just now.

- Remember, kindness from others is a powerful drug, and it will help you feel better and be stronger.

PART 2:

Challenges: negotiating the minefield

Part 2: Challenges: negotiating the minefield

2.1 Chemo, scans and other tests

Late one Friday afternoon, shortly after getting home from hospital, I received a call from a nurse at the local hospital, asking if I would please go in to see the consultant gynaecologist first thing on Monday morning.

Why a phone call late Friday afternoon for an appointment early on Monday morning? What was the rush? The nurse said it was to discuss ongoing treatment, a subject that had never previously been raised. I asked if she meant chemotherapy (that old terror of mine) and was tersely told that she could not discuss it with me over the phone. So, because of her extreme lack of empathy or even basic sensitivity, I was left to wallow in the fear of a chemo treatment discussion surfacing after the weekend. What a long, anxious weekend. The fear of not knowing or understanding the implications raised my stress levels to new heights.

True enough, on the Monday, the consultant confirmed that I would need a course of six chemotherapy sessions to make a 'belt and braces' job of annihilating any cancer seedlings that might have been lurking in the darker reaches of my body. To say I was frightened and upset is an understatement. Next up was a meeting with a new consultant, an oncologist, who explained the whole procedure, the risks, the horrendous-sounding side effects, and, crucially, the objective, which was to get me into remission.

Remission is the point where the cancer has disappeared. This is usually termed NED – no evidence of disease – after tests confirm this on completion of the chemo programme. Chemotherapy is the treatment of the disease by means of chemicals, where a specific range is available dependent on the type of cancer. Many different permutations exist to create a bespoke cocktail for the individual, and the dose is based on the type and stage of the specific cancer, as well as the height and weight of the patient. This series of treatments usually extends over many months and, it would be true to say, it is physically and psychologically draining. The physical side effects can cover nausea, headaches, bowel problems and intense fatigue. The psychological ones can include anxiety about the effectiveness of the treatment, fear of suffering, and depression about the length of and need for the treatment. Needless to say, there are many other possible side effects, and the effect on the person and body can range from low impact to high impact. Personally, I suffered from nausea and bowel problems, both of which were adequately managed through medication, though with a bit of trial and error along the way. Like many others, my first chemo programme included a drug known as paclitaxel, for which, unfortunately, one side effect is hair loss. To me this was initially very distressing. Others embrace this, seeing it on the one hand as a 'new look', and on the other hand feeling reassured the drug is having an effect. In due course I came to like the new short 'pixie' hair growth that came back a couple of months after the end of the treatment.

Scans and blood tests bring challenges of their own. There is always the stressful lead-up to the test or scan, together with the physical discomfort of the process, and then the anxiety-laden wait for results, sometimes over an agonising few weeks. Never underestimate the stress this causes; and it does not get easier with time and practice. Logic and reason hardly ever work when you are awaiting such vital answers, where the results can have life-changing outcomes. In my experience, no one handles the wait for results of scans or blood tests with implacable, phlegmatic calm! It is best to keep busy and occupied: time spent doing activities you enjoy helps a lot. Being with supportive family and loved ones can prove particularly valuable. However, at the end of the day, the inescapable reality of awaiting results can dominate every minute, if you allow it to.

Key points

- If the doctors are investing in expensive treatments such as chemotherapy or radiotherapy, then they are trying hard to help you recover. Keep that as a positive.

- The medical team legally have to tell you all the risks involved. Ask for as much information as you want or need, and ask for the positives and examples. If you do not want as much information, say so.

- Factor in a treat, or some company, on days of treatment. It will not make the treatment any different but will make you feel comforted.

- Remember, anxiety at this time is understandable and normal.

2.2 Feelings and emotions

2.2.1 Isolation

A diagnosis of cancer is an isolating experience. I am lucky to have amazingly supportive family and friends; but no matter how lucky a person is, at the end of the day it is a unique, individual diagnosis. For one person only. You. No matter how caring or motivating others can be, it is the patient alone who has to cope with the treatment and possible pain. In the early hours of a long, dark night, this feeling of isolation can seem insurmountable. Because, in truth, only the patient can go through the treatment or learn to accept the situation. It is hard; very hard. It only requires sensitive encouragement from others: no brash, jolly exhortations, but calm, caring, consistent support. No quips such as, 'Oh, it'll be fine,' because no one, not even the medics, can know what is going to happen in the future.

A sense of isolation may come in waves; it may be triggered again and again by reflection, a medical problem, or just a bad day. Patience and caring support in the form of companionship, phone calls or texts, or just being there, is the quiet strength that is needed. It is important to be aware that isolation can lead to loneliness and heighten feelings of general anxiety. This has a direct impact on emotional health and well-being.

2.2.2 Emotional health

A cancer patient, by definition, is already coping with physical ill-health. This can be compounded considerably by their state of emotional well-being, which is often not given due consideration and overlooked. In a time of struggling NHS resources, it is rare to have access to a service that supports the well-being of a cancer patient, but where such services exist, they can have a hugely beneficial impact on the patient. I had access to an Oncology Health Service within the cancer hospital in my region, and can vouch for the advantages of accessing support this way at times of great anxiety. Highly trained staff can offer a listening ear and advise on helpful techniques and coping strategies.

Some hospitals have a Maggie's Centre in their grounds (www.maggiescentres.org), providing free practical, emotional and social support to everyone with cancer and their supporters. Emotional support is a key element of their provision and this has been proven to strengthen emotional well-being at a time of anxiety, uncertainty and stress. Anxiety is a natural response to a cancer diagnosis and can flag up all sorts of issues: anxiety about coping, about test results, about having treatment or not, and anxiety can be a difficult habit to break. Just being in a supportive environment can be comforting and calming.

Similarly, fear is a corrosive emotion, wearing away even the strongest resolve. Fear of the unknown, fear of pain, fear of dying: all can have a massively detrimental effect on a patient's well-being. Anger may be in there, too – the 'Why me?' syndrome – and this anger may be deflected on to other areas or, more unfortunately, on to other people. Patients with any of these emotional issues need careful, quiet and unconditional support, yet this can be difficult for carers to cope with on an ongoing basis. This is why those centres also support family, friends and other carers.

Fear of the unknown and a lack of control can affect patient and carer alike. At times such as these, it is best to remember to take one small step at a time, one day at a time. And talk. Talk to people who care personally or professionally. Talk to a friend, or talk to the Macmillan organisation (www.macmillan.org.uk) or another medical professional. In my case I mostly talked to family members and close friends, along with the more formal access to the Oncology Health Department. I also occasionally joined in discussions online with a cancer charity that provided support and understanding. Metaphorical hand holding and reassurance went a long way toward bolstering my emotional health. If there is a hospice in your area, ask the GP for a referral to a specialist palliative counsellor. This, too, can be invaluable. So ask for help whether you are a patient or carer. The help you need is out there somewhere for you.

2.2.3 Processing the diagnosis

No one wants to hear the news that they have cancer. It is a cruel blow that leaves many of us reeling. All of a sudden, your body is harbouring an alien, a killer, which you cannot control. The shock can be devastating, and uncertainty about the future can rear its ugly head, affecting your behaviour and outlook. Disbelief, fear and anger can all come into play, and each patient will react differently and take their own time to process the unwanted diagnosis. Within a short time, a treatment plan of action will be put in place and, in my experience, this gives you back an element of control. Once you know about the way ahead, the terror can recede, although the effects can remain for some time and that dark cloud is never far away. It takes time to acknowledge that you have cancer and that you are now a cancer patient. With support, patience and time, the trauma of diagnosis can diminish. But one never forgets the moment when the news was delivered.

2.2.4 Acceptance

As I have already mentioned, coming to terms with a cancer diagnosis takes time and patience. It cannot be hurried. To accept it you must first acknowledge it and understand it. This is a tall order. Admitting and accepting to yourself that you have cancer takes courage, and I mean that most sincerely. It is such a frightening and life-changing event. Each person will have their own timetable of acceptance, with several stages they need to pass through. As well as acknowledgement and acceptance, these stages may include understanding the wider implications, including the ripple effect on others and your commitments, the financial implications, finding and using a reliable support system and, vitally, getting the panic under control. This phase can trigger a reassessment of priorities, resulting in both a shift of focus and a change in the intensity of focus. Some old priorities may be dropped, while others may gain a fiercely renewed urgency. A flexible and adaptable approach may be necessary.

Once the trauma of diagnosis and treatment has subsided, things settle back to normal. Or do they? What was normal before is no longer appropriate, so you may need to work on finding a new normal that will help you adapt to living your life with cancer. There is bereavement in the mix, too. Bereavement for a lost way of life, one that was not driven by medical appointments, and limited by surgery or medication, or low physical, or psychological, energy. Coming to terms with the 'new you' will take time and patience for everyone. But when acceptance does come to you, there will be less stress and more energy with which to build a new future. Perhaps it will not be the one you had originally planned and looked forward to, but a future nonetheless. Acceptance is an important step, and one that allows you to move forward.

2.2.5 Reflection

Learning to live with cancer changes everything. You are walking a path you have not chosen, but you must keep walking, taking one step at a time. Inevitably this requires a period of readjustment to cope with any changes needed to adapt to living with cancer. Only through reflection, after acceptance, can a new 'normal' be established. Reflecting on the situation, the limitations, the difficulties and the identification of priorities, can enable you to make progress. Reflection does not necessarily require a long period, or formal, organised thoughts. In fact, occasional snatched quiet moments can be a more natural and effective way to reflect. Odd moments occur in daily life; for example, while you are relaxing in a bath, walking the dog, or queueing for a bus. These can be spontaneous opportunities for quiet reorganisation of thought. To consider what has happened and how this will affect you, your family, your life, and your future, is a way of getting back some control. Considering your options, or new ways of living life to the full, is a powerful tool for positive change. Reflection feeds reprioritisation, and this leads to pointers or signposts for the best way forward while living with cancer.

Key points

- This is your life we're talking about. Be patient, and be kind to yourself.

- Access emotional support or well-being services where they are on offer.

- Both patients and carers need a quiet and supportive environment.

- Expect to experience a range of emotions. Try not to take your frustrations out on those nearest to you.

- Remember that acceptance and adjustment will eventually come, and you will move forward.

2.3 Planning and reprioritisation

2.3.1 Having a strategy

I have found that having a plan is halfway to gaining back some sense of control. The strategy may be tenuous, but identifying options and support is such a positive step in itself. Key to the strategy is knowing who is truly on your team. This means having a team comprising people who can be relied on, through all the ups and downs – people who love and care for you no matter what. We all know friends and acquaintances who say the right words and mean to be helpful, but do not come up with the goods when circumstances demand the right reaction. There is always a reason why they cannot be involved when they are needed. This isn't to blame them; merely to say you need to know who you can rely on when the plan goes to pot, and things change with little or no warning. Sadly, this can be a common occurrence when dealing with cancer. So a good reliable team is fundamental to your strategy.

You need to do your research. Cancer is particular to the individual, both in how it can affect a person and the treatment options that may or may not be available. There is a vast amount of information available online and in hard copies from various organisations, such as Macmillan, libraries, GP surgeries, hospitals, and a variety of specific cancer-related charities. These deal with queries ranging from financial ones, to the latest research and drugs available, and right through to help with depression. For those who do not wish, or feel unable, to go through these channels on their own, there is always someone willing to listen and provide the information on a one-to-one verbal basis. This could be a GP, a district nurse or Macmillan nurse, a library volunteer, or even a friend who would be willing to research the information you need on your behalf.

There is also a wealth of online information. However, a strong word of caution here: always use a trusted website, such as www.nhs.uk. There are also many 'bespoke' cancer forums, usually in conjunction with charities, which can be an incredible source of support. I am a member of an ovarian cancer forum where all members/contributors are either ovarian cancer patients or their carers. I find that sharing information and experiences is immensely valuable. It is interesting too, as the participants are not just regional or national, but also global. Learning how treatment is conducted in Australia, which anti-nausea medication is used in Germany, or the latest research coming out of America is fascinating, and it all adds to the wealth of information that may prove pertinent to one's own situation.

As before, you need to identify your trusted team. Once you know who you can rely on and have the relevant information to hand, you can start finding out what your options are, and will have a full-blown strategy in place. Even if it is as basic as, 'Well, if "x" happens, I can do "y",' or, 'I would like to do "z"; so, these are the steps I need to take.' Having a series of goals is life-affirming in itself. We all need things to look forward to, but they do need to be realistic.

At the time of writing, I am having chemotherapy, so although I may fervently wish to escape to the Yorkshire Dales for a few days, this is unrealistic. But I can plan to do it in a few months' time, which gives me something to aim for and look forward to. A good strategy also covers less pleasant occurrences. When I was told I would be going back onto chemo I already knew who could accompany me to the sessions to keep me occupied and support me if I were to become anxious. Plan B to the fore! I confess that the word 'strategy' does sound quite corporate, but we all know and understand the value of a good plan. Not least, it feels good to have a plan, even if it is a simple and straightforward one. So a plan is a good thing!

Reprioritisation is a slippery customer. Well, there are the inevitable decisions that take priority: 'Shall we meet our friends for coffee or do I have to attend the hospital appointment at

10.30?' Clearly that is a straightforward priority decision (or should be). Less easy is the 'Shall I start the ironing, or do we go out for a walk?' Every day becomes a balance of using time wisely while simultaneously accepting the reality of normal life and its demands. When my oncologist advised me to do those things I wanted to do, my mind went blank and nothing urgent surfaced. Wishing to go round the world on a super yacht may be at the forefront of some people's wish list, but it is rarely a realistic one and certainly not one of mine.

It is a time for reflection on what is truly important. So often in ordinary life we let time slip away and waste it on unimportant things. We squander time in general. It is only when we get that wake-up call that, hey, a lifetime really is limited, perhaps more so than we hoped, that we face the issue and decide what truly is important. Now is the time to do those things that you have always said you wanted to do. Learn to play the piano? Why not? Camp in the Cairngorms? If that is what switches you on, just do it! Spend more time with the family? Now is the perfect time to make those memories, for yourself and others. It is a balancing act, deciding what is important and what is less so. We will not always get it right, and every day cannot always be turned into a holiday (our friend, Reality, does have a role after all) but a general intention to use time wisely is the key here. One further piece of splendid advice from my oncologist was not just 'Do what you want to do' but 'Do not do what you do not want to do.' Life truly is too short to attend meetings of organisations that are no longer a priority and belong to a past existence, or to meet people you do not like or who you feel uncomfortable with. As someone once famously said, 'Life is too short to peel a grape!'

2.3.2 Diet

A lot has been written about diet for cancer sufferers. Specialist books are easily accessible through libraries or bookshops. I found publications on nutrition and diet from the Macmillan Support Service particularly helpful. In particular, I found The Royal Marsden Cancer Cookbook to be excellent (Kyle Books, 2015; edited by Dr Clare Shaw; ISBN: 978 0 85783 2320). I think that good old common sense comes into play here. It makes sense to eat a range of good fresh food, rather than a diet of chips and pastries. The occasional plate of yummy chips or a delicious Danish pastry is not the end of the world, but living on them alone is hardly conducive to a healthy body.

Much has been written about a 'rainbow diet'; that is, one that includes a lot of colourful fruit and vegetables; and plenty of good fresh food of this type can only be a good thing. Balance is of course necessary with protein, and it is considered that a wide range of foodstuffs is the best way to go. Indeed, meat is a valuable source of iron and vitamins, although having some meat-free days is now considered healthy too. A severe change of diet may not be optimal when the body is already under stress dealing with cancer and its treatments. So before making drastic changes (like becoming vegan overnight), perhaps a word with a medical advisor would be sensible. Of course, some cancers may require a change of diet, in which case a dietician from the hospital can advise on the best way to make the adjustment. And, of course, dietary adjustment may also be necessary during a course of chemotherapy. Be wary of any cancer diets, supplements or 'cures' you find online: only ever use information from valid professional sources such as the NHS, Macmillan or advice directly from your medical team. Also, be aware that some supplements may interfere with medication or chemotherapy. Always ask your doctor or nurse for specialist advice before taking supplements or significantly altering your diet.

Your sense of taste may change, particularly when on chemo, and this may influence what you want to eat. The Royal Marsden Cancer Cookbook is an invaluable resource to have to hand in the kitchen, as it offers ideas and recipes for all sorts of cancer-related issues that affect our diet and choice of foodstuffs. It includes recommendations for food to eat if you are finding it difficult to swallow, if your nausea is bad, or if specific vitamins or minerals need a boost. With all food, it is better to have a small amount of quality ingredients rather than a large amount of less nutritionally valuable food. It makes sense that if you want a healthy body, you must use healthy food to fuel it. We can all make that choice, but still have room for the occasional treat. Having the occasional glass of wine or a slice of delicious cake is not going to be your downfall unless you have been specifically advised not to do so. At the end of the day, it is all down to personal choice; and bear in mind that 'a little of what you fancy does you good!'

2.3.3 Trust

You cannot demand or buy trust: it is only ever earned. This means trust in your medical team, trust in your personal support team, and trust in your own decisions. Trust in the medical team is vital. Are they experts in your cancer field? Do they communicate well with you? Do they have the patience to explain everything? Do you trust them with your life? This last question is the key one, because that is exactly what you are being asked to do, and trust does not get much more important than that. Trust in your personal team has already been covered to some extent, as you have already identified those people who care about you and will stand up to be counted when the occasion demands it. We do not always get the right team in place first time round. However, through experience we find those people whom we can trust to be there for us.

Trusting in ourselves and our own decisions is not so easy. But if we can say that our decision was the right one at the time, with the knowledge we had in those particular circumstances, then that is the best we can hope for. It is all well and good to be wise after the event. If a decision turns out to be wrong later on, it must be put down as one of life's less successful experiences. If you are able to learn something, then do so. That is the important part.

If I decide to go shopping, for example, and it turns out that I get too tired, then I store that information to use when I have a similar decision to make in the future, and hope that I judge my abilities better next time round! No mistake or misjudgement is ever wasted if it can count as a learning experience.

Trust is not an easy thing to define, but when you have trust in something or someone, it is a valuable asset to have in coping with life. Personally, when I am faced with a big decision, I tend to defer to someone who knows better than me, rather than trust the limitations of my own knowledge. For instance, if a doctor asks me for a decision between treatment A and treatment B, I ask them what they would advise their sister/aunt to do and, equally important, why they would make that choice. Or I ask what the pros and cons are, so that the decision becomes clearer. Certainly, use other people as sounding boards, and take as much time as is needed or available for the decision-making process. But always remember two things: that this is your decision and you ultimately have the final say. So trust yourself too.

2.3.4 Recurrence

Once you have been diagnosed with cancer, and had the appropriate treatment, it is common to live in fear of a recurrence. In many cases, once the surgery and/or treatment has finished, that is thankfully the end of the problem. But in some cases (my own is a prime example), the cancer can recur. It may, or may not, reappear in the same place; it can also jump ship and turn up in random places. This brings a fear like no other. For example, in my case the tumour was in the ovary, but it has reappeared at the back of the stomach, the pelvis, and on the liver. It likes to spread its favours around, obviously. This came as quite a blow, despite my knowing that it could happen. Without wanting to overcomplicate the story, my breast cancer and the ovarian cancer were not linked, although one might be forgiven for thinking that they could be. Both were hormone-related cancers, but totally independent. I was also offered genetic testing to see how it might affect my family, but there was no gene mutation, which is uncommon where both breast and ovarian cancer are present. As one medic casually remarked, 'You've just been unlucky.' Such an understatement of the palpably obvious, is arguably insensitive. Either way, it is most certainly not an easy thing to hear when your life is literally at stake.

When cancer recurs, it can be tested to see if it is 'secondary'; that is, whether there is a definite pathological link to the first cancer. In my case, ovarian cancer is a hormonal cancer, which means that it is transported around the body by the blood system. Wherever it recurs, blood tests can identify its origin, which in turn helps target the appropriate treatment. Constantly thinking about and living with the worry of a recurrence is just one more aspect of a cancer diagnosis that one has to learn to manage and live with. It is not easy.

This is why waiting for results of regular, maintenance scans and tests can be such a very anxious time. There is always that 'What if?' moment or two, when it is so easy to think the worst. However, when thinking the worst, it is sometimes useful to ask yourself, 'What evidence do I have for thinking the worst?' 'Is that ache a new symptom, or is it just my age?' It is so easy to jump to conclusions. Being overly sensitive and predisposed to misinterpreting an ache or pain as the first sign of the cancer returning is all completely understandable in these circumstances. Of course, it is only natural that patients will worry and, in particular, be anxious if there appear to be any new pains or symptoms. That is human nature after all.

Other situations that may trigger anxiety include news about someone else with cancer, where their distress may cause flashbacks or difficult memories. The anticipation of a medical appointment can also cause a lot of stress and worry about the outcome. Talking openly to someone about these fears can soften the impact and also alert others to how you are feeling. Being part of a support group is extremely helpful, as is sharing concerns with any medical professional or counsellor. The important thing to remember is that anxiety after your cancer diagnosis and treatment is a natural, if uncomfortable, reaction. And if a recurrence is eventually confirmed, then, a bit like a game of Snakes and Ladders, you go back to the beginning again. So get a support team and a plan. Oh, so easy to say or write, but oh so difficult to put into place. You need patience, strength and time. However, it can be done. I am living proof of that.

Key points

- Having a plan or strategy will give you an element of control and make you feel more positive.

- Use only trusted and validated resources, whether books, communities or online.

- Eat a good quality diet, but also have room for occasional treats.

- Work out who you can rely on, and trust in your own judgement.

- Accept the fact that the thought of recurrence is frightening yet understandable. Learn to accept the worry and manage it.

- Remember, living with cancer is difficult but, with your trusted team, you will cope.

PART 2: CHALLENGES: NEGOTIATING THE MINEFIELD

1 April 1967 – Mark: Carolyn was only 20 years old when she got married to David. David would have waited until Carolyn's twenty-first birthday later that summer but Carolyn was determined to have a spring wedding without delay!

1 April 2017 – Mark: Still in love on their golden wedding anniversary outside the church doors through which they had taken some of their first steps as a married couple. No regrets. Timeless love.

Summer 2004 At home with 'the girls' and the daffodils. After bringing up a family, I went back to work, initially volunteering at the local hospice in the Bereavement Support Office, gaining a Diploma in Counselling and Therapy before my career in Higher Education took off. When I retired, I was Head of the University's Academic Skills Development Service, and by later that year, I had completed a Doctorate in Educational Policy. As I said, not a bad record for a late starter!

19 April 2009 – One of 'the girls' in Scotland looking as captivated by the daffodils as I was. Scotland is magical, not just because David and I spent our honeymoon and often took holidays there, but because of the glorious landscape and friendly people. By 2014, I had started organising an annual trip to Scotland for a group of friends, but due to my first course of chemotherapy in 2015, was unable to go that year. [Mark: Carolyn made it back the following year and visited for the last time in 2018.]

7 June 2014 – David was President of the local Rotary club in 2014. Shortly after this photo of the four of us was taken, David and I went on the holiday to Scotland from which we returned to find the letter about my mammogram recall that changed my life. This is the last photo of the four of us before my cancer diagnosis. The second photo completes my team, all five of us; it's just that some of us were more informal than others …

25 March 2015 – One of my last visits to my favourite view point before starting my first round of chemotherapy. I had previously had radiotherapy and kept my hair – I dreaded losing my hair. [Mark: For Christmas in 2019, which was Carolyn's last, she received a 1m x 0.4m framed photo of the view so that, even on the tough days, she would be able to see her favourite view.]

28 April 2015 – This shows me wearing a wig after my first course of chemotherapy. I confess I favoured a more natural look over the luminous green bob, rainbow Mohican and long black Louis IV curls (complete with goatee!) sent to me by one of my sons. You have to keep the ability to see the humour in life, which can be easier said than done.

28 August 2015 – Mark: Carolyn, happy at having made it through the first round of chemotherapy and recovering her complexion – she had been very pale and gaunt during the final doses of chemo. After she had lost her hair, it grew back, to Carolyn's great surprise, much softer than it had ever been before. Also, at this time, one friend had found 'a little bag of happiness' (look it up on the internet) and sent it to Carolyn. It was a huge boost for her.

2 October 2015 – Mark: Just getting out of the house for some fresh air felt like such a treat. Carolyn had grown up by the sea and always loved walking along the beach. Although it is not very visible, her hair had started to grow back.

From mid-2016 through 2017, Carolyn started saving sayings she came across that she would often reread, and draw strength from – perhaps you, or someone you know, may draw strength from them too.

'Expecting life to treat you well because you are a good person is like expecting an angry bull not to charge because you are a vegetarian.'

Shari R. Barr, author

'On particularly rough days when I am sure I can't possibly endure, I like to remind myself that my track record for getting through bad days so far is 100%. And that is pretty good.'

Michelle Weidenbenner, author, Fractured Not Broken

'You never know how strong you are until being strong is the only choice you have.'

Bob Marley, singer, songwriter and musician

'You are strong for getting out of bed in the morning when it feels like hell. You are brave for doing things even though they scare you or make you anxious. And you are amazing for trying and holding on no matter how hard life gets.'

www.tinybuddha.com

'I'll never get back to my pre-cancer self. She died somewhere along the way. This reborn version of my self is proving tenacious and daring!'

Anonymous

'Sometimes in life you just need a hug. No words, no advice, just a hug to make you feel better.'

www.tinybuddha.com

'Courage doesn't always roar. Sometimes courage is the little voice at the end of the day that says I'll try again tomorrow.'

Mary Anne Radmacher, writer and artist

25 December 2019 – Mark: Mum's last Christmas. By early autumn 2019, the most appropriate treatment options were no longer proving effective. Mum nevertheless wanted to try the next best option, which the doctor's thought would not work. But it surprised us all, and gave Mum one last Christmas.

29 May 2020 – Mark: More chemo. Carolyn was determined to celebrate even small wins. Yet two months after this photograph was taken, she knew her 'less effective' chemotherapy was losing its effectiveness on the cancer and ultimately decided to stop her treatment. In July 2020 Carolyn decided to stop the fight – that was truly brave but she felt this was right for her. After years of sickness, Carolyn wanted quality over quantity – see her stare below: there is clearly more behind her eyes than her smile.

6 September 2020 – Mark: A difficult time: the effectiveness of the final treatment had failed; the symptoms were sharply increasing and Carolyn was discussing quality versus quantity of life. As she sits, the strain is clearly visible.

October 2020 – Mark: The final picture of Carolyn in October 2020. From the beginning of November onwards, Carolyn's condition rapidly deteriorated, and she was admitted to the same hospice she had volunteered at many years previously. Carolyn passed away peacefully there in December 2020.

A Time to Just . . . Be.

PART 3:

A creative strategy

Part 3: A creative strategy

A successful plan or strategy needs to be well thought through. Be kind and patient with yourself when you start. It has to be flexible, realistic, reliable and quick to action. This is also the opportunity to think outside the box. Do not be afraid to be creative. A good start is to break down the strategy into its component parts. But what does a good plan cover? What are the needs of the individual? What would be helpful or advisable? I would suggest that a plan includes those items that could loosely be put under the following headings: practical, emotional, behavioural and spiritual.

3.1 Practical: support the body's healing through nutrition and exercise

In times of illness and crisis, practical help is invaluable. As I said earlier, some friends are more comfortable doing something, rather than talking: they prefer taking action to providing emotional support. So visiting and bringing a cake or a casserole is a perfect solution that gives them the satisfaction that they are helping their friend with something practical and worthwhile. There may be neighbours who will happily bring some shopping when they do their own, or walk the dog occasionally; they only need asking. People like to feel needed and valued, yet at the same time they do not want to intrude. I find asking for favours difficult as it can feel like an admittance of weakness or failure, but it is something we need to understand and accept; accepting help is actually more a sign of strength.

Having help in the house may also be an option. This can be arranged through Social Services, perhaps via the GP's surgery, or through a private arrangement, depending on your circumstances. A once-a-week clean, tidy and bed-linen wash, especially in the early weeks of treatment or post-surgery, could make a huge difference.

Medical equipment may also be borrowed from the NHS Health Trust. This might include a walking stick, commode or shower stool, which would help with the initial weakness and vulnerability. The services of the district nurse in the community are vital in supporting patients. District nurses can help with dressings and injections, and provide important hand-holding at the same time, while offering every medical skill in between. They are a great source of support, advice and confidence building.

Family and friends may also be called on for lifts to hospital or other appointments. There is usually a facility for hospital transport, but providing a lift can be a good way for people to help those they care about. Car parking at some hospitals is free for cancer patients and their drivers, so this can make it easier all round too.

You may need financial advice; this can usually be facilitated by the Macmillan service. They have published a booklet on getting help with financial issues relating to cancer and provide pointers on where to access help that is beyond their remit. Social Services can also be approached for advice – check your GP's surgery too, even if they do not have anything helpful, they may be able to suggest where to find information. If you are still working, then stay directly in touch with the Human Resources manager or your boss to keep them updated on your situation. You will also find out what to expect from them financially during the immediate future. It is imperative to remove this uncertainty.

This may also be the time to look at any legal documents that need updating, such as a will, or expression of wishes, and an opportunity to put into place those things we all put off indefinitely. Contact the Law Society (www.lawsociety.org.uk) for information on solicitors in your area, or simple pre-made wills are available to buy from some stationers and online. Moreover, knowing where you stand in relation to financial commitments, such as mortgages, will give peace of mind when there are so many other things going on. Assessing and understanding all the outgoings and incomings of financial life, and getting them in healthy order, will leave you time and space for focussing on getting as well as you can.

3.2 Emotional: decrease stress, particularly emotional stress, and have a trusted support team

It is so important to be able to express how you feel to others. Bottling up negative emotions is harmful: there has to be a safety valve somewhere in your life. This emotional release can be with family members, friends, medical professionals, counsellors, Macmillan contacts or others. It may feel easier to express yourself in writing rather than vocally, from noting down emotional feelings in a notebook to writing to a friend. It can be surprising how cathartic it is to see and read what lands on paper once you start writing. Or you may feel more comfortable talking to a stranger. Only you will know, and each time it may need a different outlet.

I have used most of these ideas at some stage, with varied results, depending on the state I was in. For example, I was initially advised to go to a well-respected palliative counsellor at the local hospice; but on that occasion, it really did not work for me. The second time I tried it, with his younger colleague, it was much better and highly effective. So do not give up at the first hurdle. As well as Macmillan, other charities offer a listening service on a one-to-one basis, which may be particularly suitable if you need an element of emotional distance. I also valued talking to close friends and church ministers, but this may not be for everyone. I confess, I often tried not to be over-emotional and flood the priest or vicar with lots of tears. Sometimes when the tsunami of emotion overwhelms us (and I speak from personal experience) the best thing is to have time out and just 'BE'. We all need space, quiet and time for self-reflection, and this can only be done in a safe, gentle environment.

3.3 Behavioural: count blessings, give life meaning, and a new purpose. Create a new normal.

I have touched on the changed reality for cancer sufferers. Inevitably this leads to changes in behaviour as we adjust to the new life that we now find ourselves leading. Changes in routine or expectation can challenge the best of us at the best of times, and some people find this incredibly difficult to adjust to. Once again, use every trick in the book to help yourself cope as you take on new patterns of lifestyle. Try to create a positive environment so that negative influences, whether they be people or routines, are kept to a minimum. That is easier said than done, but prioritising what we enjoy and what is good for us should also enable good behaviours to develop, as we will be more relaxed and readier to deal with new daily events, issues or just plain old challenges!

Exercise is good for us. I am not talking doing a marathon here, or any need to invest in a costly gym subscription. Gentle regular exercise is known to be more valuable than intense, inconsistent bursts of enthusiasm. Art therapy can be useful and is sometimes available in the more resourceful hospitals. Just dabbling with some paint on paper at home can be a release for emotions. It can be astonishing what can be produced with little artistic training or aptitude. Music has long been known to affect mood, whether it is lively, stimulating pop music, or soothing, classical music that can lower blood pressure and certainly relax the body and mind.

And what about the bucket list? Our behaviour needs to reflect our great wake-up call. Perhaps this is the perfect time to be creative? Surprise yourself, as well as others. Channel your energy, limited though it may be, into something new. This is great for brain health, as new connections are made and the brain is exercised at the same time. This will be a 'new you', so feel bold enough to create a new life and learn new and interesting skills. Moreover, if you meet new people, they will not be comparing you to the 'old you'. Woodworking, photography, creative writing, a new language or watercolour painting – just go for it. Now is the time to do things you have never had the time for before. Being creative while living with cancer can have a dual role – as well as developing new skills, there is the benefit of a welcome distraction and something more positive to process. This makes a difference both physically and psychologically. The stimulus of new things will boost your overall well-being in so many positive ways.

This leads me neatly on to the issue of treats. I have decided that now is not the time to deny myself a treat. Whether your special treat is a piece of velvety chocolate, a slice of yummy cake, or a chilled glass of Chablis every evening – whether it is treating yourself to a weekly bunch of flowers, or an overnight stay in a favourite country pub, break the strict habits of a disciplined lifetime and just enjoy it. Remember, one can always regret things one has done: that is part of life. But it is far worse to regret those things that we did not do when we had the chance to do them. Do not waste valuable time revisiting old regrets: time is too precious. Move forward slowly to new opportunities and appreciate the positivity they bring.

3.4 Spiritual: beliefs, religion, meditation

The spirituality of a person can become more evident at times of personal crisis or trauma, and certainly during life-changing events; particularly if it involves facing our own mortality. Spirituality is a broad topic that can be interpreted in a multitude of ways. Generally speaking, it involves looking for a deeper understanding of the meaning of life. Spirituality differs from religion or some sort of personal connection with something greater than ourselves, in that it is a quest for understanding rather than a belief system. Spiritual values encompass the human values of truth, peace, righteousness, and non-violence. These are common denominators of various aspects of religion that can be found in the teachings of Christianity, Judaism, Buddhism and Islam. Accessing one's own spirituality can happen through being in places of worship such as churches or other religious buildings, other places of peace and quiet or, indeed, the natural environment. This process can be facilitated by priests or other religious leaders, the hospital chaplaincy team or, more simply, with friends who have the understanding and ability to support you in your spiritual development.

Non-religious spirituality involving the values outlined above can include learning to love yourself as well as others. Perhaps start a diary or journal identifying everything you are grateful for, or positive actions that have happened during the day. Try to help others through your actions and words. A spiritual person cares about people and animals and seeks to protect the world in general. Spending time outdoors in the natural environment can be both soothing and inspiring. Importantly, spiritual people learn to forgive others and forgo negativity or destructive thoughts. This will bring a sense of calm.

Other ways to seek a better understanding can be accessed through books, apps and TV or radio programmes. You may find meditation useful, either practising alone or learning a guided technique in an organised group. There is a wealth of information and help out there for you to consider. These techniques can inspire confidence and calm, which may lead to a greater understanding of oneself and one's place in the world, and to develop a personal acceptance of the meaning of life and ultimately the ending of it.

Key points

- **Practical:** If necessary, get help with shopping, cleaning, appointments and finances.

- **Emotional:** Talk to a friend or professional; write things down or keep a journal.

- **Behavioural:** Accept changes are inevitable as you adjust to the situation. Take appropriate exercise, and take up a new hobby. Make time for a treat or two!

- **Spiritual:** Learn to be kind to yourself and others. Peace, acceptance and calm will follow.

- **Remember:** do not waste time looking back; look forward to new things.

Bonus benefit

Daydreaming

This is the most pleasurable bit. It is the mood I sneak into whenever the urge takes me. It is relaxing, stress-busting, and positive, and releases all-important endorphins for the feel-good factor. This is a great way of spending time, letting the rigid shoulders relax and soften – and it can be great fun! Daydreaming can be about anything you want it to be – sit down, put your feet up and escape into your daydreams.

Personally, I pick up my trusty iPad and look up the sweetest, comfiest cottage to escape to, or an elegant spacious home that would be perfect to go to for a break with family or close friends. I look at travelogues and imagine myself at the heady heights of Machu Picchu, or soaking up the amazingly atmospheric Taj Mahal. I see myself travelling through the outback in Australia, all shimmering red earth and the unmistakable smell of sizzling BBQs. Or it might just be paddling in a babbling stream under the dappled shade of English willows, and retiring to a picture-postcard pub for a delicious lunch. I even imagine the menu!

You do not need technology for daydreaming either, and you can do it anywhere and at any time to suit you and your mood. You could pick up a magazine or travel brochure but, best of all, just trawl through your own imagination. Think of a time when you were really happy, and go from there. Anything that makes you relax has got to be a good thing! Just let go, and escape into your dream world, wherever it takes you. And feel the benefit . . .

Tap into your fond memories. It is so beneficial to remember and relive the good times. Times when you were happy, times when you had fun, and times that were truly memorable. Recalling these times increases the levels of serotonin in the body, contributing to feelings of relaxation, happiness and well-being. Equally, it is important to make new memories. These will help to see you through any dark days ahead, and your family and friends will remember them with fondness in the future. These are priceless benefits.

PART 4:

Conclusion

Part 4: Conclusion

4.1 Acknowledgement and acceptance is the hardest part of all

Cancer at any age or at any stage is life-threatening, so being diagnosed is extremely frightening. We probably haven't thought about it much beforehand, and certainly not in relation to our own bodies. It may take time, a lot of time, to acknowledge the profound effect this will have on our lives and the lives of those close to us. But after the initial shock and trauma, acknowledgement will come, and eventually, acceptance. A feeling of vulnerability may remain, but also an inner strength may surface, one that you did not know was there. There is a sleeping giant deep within you who responds when circumstances arouse it.

4.2 Be creative and resilient

This is the time to prioritise, sort the 'wheat from the chaff' and use time wisely. The confines and limitations of treatment and how well you feel will sharpen your focus on what is important to you and your loved ones. Motivation and determination are strong drivers that enable you to achieve things, perhaps involving the help and support of others. Let the creative juices flow, be brave and try to do what you want; have something to aim for. Keep trying, keep strong, even if it is only one small step at a time, whether managing to get through the day, the morning, or even just the next hour.

4.3 The cancer path is personal

We all need to make individual choices and we learn from all of them. There is no set pattern or prescription that suits all. It is a tangled and stony path through a maze of many stops and blind bends. But, with our trusty team alongside us, it is possible to navigate our individual route through the myriad of decisions and options that will come our way along this rough path. Talking, and sharing our thoughts and decisions with others, will cause us to reflect on these decisions as we tentatively plan our way forward. Always be prepared to alter course, that way we will know how much we have progressed on our route. The ultimate outcome may not change but the way there may be easier.

4.4 Developing medical students' understanding

Consultants and oncologists are highly trained doctors, experts in their specific medical field. But a key part of this is an understanding of patients and their psychological needs, usually acquired through years of experience. These specialists were once mere medical students, fresh-faced and eager to learn. It is imperative that they be trained at medical school to understand the emotions that may accompany a cancer diagnosis as well as to appreciate the colossal psychological impact on any cancer patient's mind once such a diagnosis has been delivered. I am talking here of a whole module on the subject, not a mere tick-box exercise vaguely covering the fundamentals. It should never be underestimated how significantly a patient's psychological and emotional reaction can affect their overall well-being. I implore all medical schools to place patient well-being at the highest level of priority, and that has to include mental well-being too. We must have ongoing development and learning in this frequently overlooked, but vitally important, area of health.

PART 4: CONCLUSION

PART 5:

A final word and message

Part 5: A final word and message

So where does that leave me in the great scheme of things? Well, when I started this book I was on a second six-month course of chemotherapy. Shortly afterwards, I was told that it had not worked. This came as a huge blow and took some time to get my head around. The oncologist was blunt, saying my options were now very limited and, indeed, I might only have months to live. He referred me to the Palliative Medicine team who tried their best to be helpful. However, a series of unanticipated circumstances involving illness, hospital admission, oncology staff changes and a fortuitous appointment with a leading globally, renowned ovarian oncologist ended in my switching consultants and hospitals. Fortunately, this leading consultant, together with the previous and new consultants, all advocated the same route, and ultimately helped to influence my decision. Thus, a few weeks later, I embarked on a new programme of weekly chemo. Quite a tough order, but one I was determined to try. Yet another twisty and bumpy section of the path I did not want to be on!

There was a lot of talk, particularly with the Palliative Care team, on the quality-versus-quantity debate, which I found horrendously difficult to navigate. How on earth do you choose between, on the one hand, stopping the treatment, the focus of which is to contain the cancer, and, on the other hand, not giving up the fight or the chance to live longer? The first option would leave me in more relative comfort, but also leave the cancer free to aggressively progress, and as a result I would have a shorter life expectancy. The second option leaves me constantly subject to illness and debilitating side effects. I made my decision to go ahead with more chemo purely based on the fact that I could not just sit back and wait to die. I felt stopping treatment and doing nothing was not an option. I would not say I was a 'fighter', but I am determined to do everything in my power to stay alive! I chose to move forward and try to buy myself some more time. I hoped that, during this extended period, other options might present themselves: perhaps new drugs would be researched, trialled, approved and become available.

What I had not envisaged was the nightmare situation of the Covid-19 virus surfacing and becoming a huge global threat at the same time. Not least, this pandemic was particularly threatening to vulnerable people of all ages whose immune system had been compromised by chemotherapy. This was a devastatingly frightening situation to find ourselves in. In turn, this raised more questions that needed the right answer. No second chances. The main question was how to balance the benefit of chemo against the increasing risk of getting the virus. A weakened immune system, together with regular trips to hospital, which was a potential breeding ground for the virus, where virus patients were being cared for, was a combination to be avoided if at all possible. A triple whammy.

Nothing can prepare you to answer those questions. They are not answered easily or satisfactorily. So as I write, I am taking a break from chemo in the hope that I will recommence it when the virus is more under control. That way I will hopefully benefit from the treatment already undertaken, which has hopefully been effective in delaying the growth. Gradually I will improve my level of immunity to cope with any infection that may come my way, and it may provide time for the threat of the virus to come under better control, and drugs to be developed to reduce the risk to vulnerable patients. Importantly this may help to reduce the pressure on our valiant NHS staff. It is a balancing act like no other.

These are truly unprecedented, surreal times. For those of us already fighting for our lives this adds a dimension of scary proportions. But we cancer patients have already shown determination and an ability to keep going along this difficult path, against all the odds. So we must keep going forward, one small step at a time, put a smile on our faces and enjoy every element of living that we can. We must count our blessings and face each day with hope. Some days this will be a very tough call indeed. Life is often unfair, but we are here, and we are alive. We might not have chosen this path to go down, but the fact remains that we are on it, and we should value every minute and every kindness we encounter. We can use the time to live in the moment, for the benefit not only of ourselves but also our loved ones. It is a time to just BE.

PART 6:

Involving other people

Part 6: Involving other people

6.1 A note from a friend

Experience has taught me that, every now and then, if you are lucky, you come across someone so compatible in their thinking, humour and understanding that you hardly remember a time when they were not there. Carolyn is such a friend to me. To know the agony that cancer has brought to her has given me the chance to show how much I care. From the first moment of hearing about the illness, nothing was ever about me in this story of a fight for survival.

I do not know how my dear friend feels and I do not know what lies ahead. All I have been able to do is to offer my loving friendship, and to listen carefully to all her words – and sometimes the heart-breaking absence of them, when I have heard instead the breathless fight for control over such terror. I have prayed for her, especially when I know she faces another hurdle (the next scan, cancer-marker test results, more surgery, more chemo and the impact on her increasingly frail body), and I have also tried to make her laugh.

So if you have a friend like mine, you can stand up to be counted when you are needed. I was lucky to be needed. This is my responsibility, but, above all, my privilege. I am part of her team. While she tries to just 'be', I will just be there.

6.2 A note from a minister

Carolyn and I have chosen to walk alongside each other on life's meandering pathway over some decades now. I would say we have a 'meeting of minds' both academically and spiritually, which has proved a tremendous blessing to us both. Some years our paths have touched at different points and less frequently; at other times we have worked and walked very closely together. It is through the dark times that my friend and I have so come to value each other's qualities of mind.

Courage and encouragement, faith and fortitude have strengthened that bond of friendship and mutual support between us. My friend's fortitude during times of crisis has been humbling to witness and her ability to aid other sufferers, despite her own struggles, has been inspiring. Her resilience and ability to see glimmers of hope even amid her own severe trials has led her to write A Path Not Chosen: Walking in a Cancer World. The unique perspective in this book will offer solace and hope, encouragement and advice. It will be invaluable to cancer sufferers everywhere.

I am so proud of you dear friend.

6.3 A son's perspective

6.3.1 Approach

When Mum first told me she wanted to write a handbook for living with cancer, she expressed the desire that it should be a practical guide, with hints and tips. She wanted to write the type of guide she wished she could have had for living in her brave new cancer world. It was a great idea. So when she asked me to write something from my point of view, I wanted to take the same approach. Here, then, is a son's perspective.

6.3.2 Context

Cancer is like a stone being thrown into a pond. There is the area of greatest impact, the point at which the pebble hits the water, and the shattered natural state and flow of the water surface. But there are also ripples: little waves radiating out from the point of impact, carrying their message outwards to all in their path. Often quiet, these insidious waves radiate their smothering and suffocating effect long after the initial splash. As devastating as a cancer diagnosis is for any human being, there is also another collateral impact. And it does not happen to the patient.

If you are as close to a cancer diagnosis as is humanly possible without receiving one yourself, the chances are that you may lose someone who does not just mean something to you, but means the world to you, or, is your entire world. This is not about living with cancer; this is about living with someone who is living with cancer. As well as there being a path not chosen for the cancer patient, it is important to acknowledge the impact of cancer on carers and tell their side of the story too.

Typically, just like the patient, you have little or no knowledge of cancer, and what it means for the days to come. But she has turned to you for support. You are the support or you are the carer.

The first thing to know is that you have absolutely no control – whether you like it or not. You are powerless. Utterly powerless. In all but one respect, you are a spectator. How you react is the determining factor of success or failure, and it is all down to you. Failing is not a choice that is open to you, so pucker up buttercup.

There will be tears; there will be fear, panic and sickness. You are not the person she turns to because you can fix things or answer her questions; you are there because she needs you. So you have to do this, and do this well. That is the bad news. The good news is that I emphasise the 'you' part in that sentence. You have already succeeded by turning up. Do not try or fuss excessively: just be you.

There is, of course, more that you can do. One Christmas, on a routine hospital visit, I hung back to ask for the candid views of my mothers' relevant medical professionals. They told me, 'She's got two to three months max' and 'Don't be surprised if she doesn't leave hospital.' That brought into sharp focus the much softer medical advice she had been given. I knew she did not want to know any timescale. It was up to me not to let my guard down, so that my mother would never know anything was untoward with her own son. That was how and why I controlled how I reacted. You can only control how you react – or try to. That was my default starting point in how I approached being with Mum on her journey.

What follows is my experience, journey, thoughts and views on what more can practically be done – it has a patient sample size of only one, and I really do not want that to change.

6.3.3 From the beginning

The first thing I remember is disbelief. The disbelief quickly gave way to anger after I first heard of my mother's diagnosis.

I was angry, extremely angry, and for a while I did not understand my own emotional reaction. I was angry at this thing, this disease: how dare it threaten my mum's life, threaten to take my mum, my mum, away from me? I just wanted to protect her, put my arms around her and tell her everything would be OK – just as she had done for me countless times when I was young, all those years ago.

The thing is, throughout all the ups and downs over my life, two elements have always been there. I have been very lucky that for nearly half a century there has always been my mum and my dad. My relationship with my father has always been that of a man's man, a professional and shared love of a dram – and over the course of the past six years since my mum's diagnosis, we have grown much closer. He is a great father, who inspires me, and I continue to learn from him. But my relationship with my mum has always been intuitively close.

Through their words and actions, my parents have taught me the importance of family – and we are a close family. Our loyalty to each other is absolute, unconditional, irrevocable and without limitation. Absolutely always do your best for your family, without any condition or expectation of any benefit. Never stop being there for them, however long it may take; and, there is no limit to how many times you will be there for them. The foundation of these values is, of course, love. It takes a lot of patience, hard work and self-sacrifice on all sides. It certainly does not mean you do not have differences of opinion; every family does – but if you have people around you who embody those core values, it matters in the difficult times. I have been unbelievably lucky to have been brought up with those core values – which made for a very close familial bond. Those close bonds make you feel strong. I do not know why I remember it so clearly, but many years ago, when the late comedian Les Dawson was interviewed about the loss of his wife of 26 years, he talked about his family, saying, 'You can face anything with love.'

My mum's support network was primarily her family, but there were some close friends too. The key thing is having that network of support – it does not have to be family. It can be anyone. But you need a network. Reach out to those you know and find out if they are going to be a support to you and part of your network. Being authentic about the situation, to yourself and others, can be hard, but you have to do it. The hardest part I found was admitting how vulnerable I felt, and how her diagnosis affected me. You will soon find out whether a person is in your network if they give you their time, and actually listen, and do so without judgement or advice – unless it is asked for. If it is, look for those who consistently provide advice that is in your best interest. Whether listening to you on the phone or, better yet, proactively offering ways to help, look for those who give you their time unconditionally. Hold on to those who do.

Be prepared for a few surprises along the way in terms of who steps forward to support you, and the way they do it. Family may be there – or not. Friends too. It really sorts out those whom you can rely on from those you cannot. One of Mum's friends, if called upon, and at absolutely no notice, is quite prepared to grab her car keys immediately the telephone call ends and drive hundreds of miles to be beside Mum. Wow!

There are also those with whom you may feel you have nothing in common any more or where there has not been a strong, or even cordial, relationship in the past – yet nonetheless, support does emerge. It is a strange, yet beautifully human condition. The complete opposite of cancer – adversity really can bring out the best in some people.

Many people will say, and no doubt mean, 'If there is anything I can do, just say it.' I guess sometimes family, friends and acquaintances either do not want to intrude or find it difficult to talk socially with someone who has cancer, given the particularly gargantuan elephant in the room. Others however take a different path. My octogenarian father, whose culinary prowess extends to bacon and eggs plus (slightly burnt) toast, has on occasion returned from visiting Mum in hospital or at the hospice to a shepherd's pie left anonymously on the back doorstep. Or an apple pie. Or another meal. How thoughtful. What wonderful and practical support – to make sure he had one good meal. Solid gold. It is truly an awe-inspiring testimony to the humanity in some people.

So do work on your support network as soon as you can. Be authentic with them, and expect a few surprises, both good, and less than what you would hope for. It is a worthwhile investment of your time before you and the cancer patient are facing your biggest challenges in living with cancer.

6.3.4 Oncologist appointments

After she was diagnosed, Mum never wanted to complete a bucket-list whirlwind tour of all seven continents. She wanted what she had always wanted: to be with, surrounded by, her family. Her only goal in life had been to be a mum, and boy, did she bat that one out of the park and then some. But with her diagnosis there were things that I could do to live up to those family values and support her.

Yes, this included always being available on the phone – and calling to check in regularly every day or other day; it did not have to be long. I also saw Mum on FaceTime, texted and WhatsApped too, but FaceTime was best. If she ever called me during the working day, I knew it was significant; so I'd drop out of work meetings immediately when I saw it was her calling. I did not share my mother's diagnosis with my workplace colleagues, as I viewed my work and non-work life as separate from each other. But if Mum called, I made my excuses and left, regardless of how important the meeting was or whether it involved superiors. I just did not give them an option. After brief apologies, I explained, 'This is important, I have to take it,' as my phone rang. I do not recall ever being pulled up on it. I guess they got the message, but if they had done – well, it is a personal matter.

There were the hospital visits too. I went every day she was in hospital if I could; although sometimes this was not possible. I attended only a few consultants' appointments with her (and Dad), almost as a personal assistant, to hear the latest news and diagnosis. This all sounds straightforward, but it takes time, even if the cancer patient is geographically close. Normally Mum was nearly 300 miles away.

Mum was a nervous wreck, a rabbit in the headlights every time she had an appointment. Who the hell would not be?!

Each time, every time, she went to find out whether the executioner's axe was about to fall: whether death was just around the corner. I cannot even begin to comprehend what that must actually, truly, feel like, and hope you and I never do.

Dad went to all the appointments. He was talismanic in support. He is a quiet bull of a man, who does not like the limelight and is very hard to dissuade if he has his sights fixed on a particular course of action. Throughout his life he has been passionate about and consumed by two things: aeroplanes and Mum. Of course, Mum won, although this was not always immediately obvious; especially if a Tiger Moth was flying within sight or earshot. But with Mum's illness, no matter what it took to support her, if he needed to redouble his efforts, he would triple them. If he needed to triple the effort, he would quadruple it. But that came at a price – do not forget that those supporting someone may need support themselves. If you are supporting both a cancer patient and another supporter, it is just as important that you also build in time with your network. It is vital. As a supporter you simply cannot afford to struggle – that is the road to failure and we are never going to go there. So pace yourself, and build in some me-time for yourself. Physically and emotionally. I struggled with the latter. I still do.

Unless your consultant's appointment is the first appointment of the day, it will probably be delayed from the scheduled time. Waiting, including the in situ delay, is very difficult – you cannot sugar-coat that. But once you get into the appointment, time will speed up and can race by because of the difficult subject matter, and the complicated challenge of simultaneously getting to grips with unfamiliar medical terms or the subtleties of particular definitions. There needs to be consideration of the pros and cons of different treatment options, all while the appointment is bathed irrepressibly in a smothering maelstrom of emotions, because, literally, a life is at stake. Time simultaneously stands still and flies by.

Sometimes Mum would come out of her appointment and still have questions. Trying to follow up on residual questions via the consultant's secretary or Mum's doctor was not always an easy or quick process. So if you find yourself in a similar position, be prepared.

Statistics about cancer produce a benchmark for society, but what is important to know is the fact that cancer is a very individual disease, very personal to the sufferer; over time, the sufferer finds their own benchmark. A low cancer marker test result for one patient could be high for another. Individual context is everything; so at least a couple of days before you go for a consultant's appointment, write up a list of questions – and be as tailored as you can. Think about everything you want to ask. Do not hold back – in fact the questions you are most worried about and you want to hold back on need to be the first questions you ask, because they are likely to be the ones that will linger in a cancer patient's head long after the appointment has finished. With the patient, work through anticipated answers, options or scenarios, and what one thing versus another means. It is not always easy.

You may need help to compare different treatments, or approaches to treatments. You need to consider the practical realities of the side effects on the patient (from sickness and hair loss to restrictions in diet: what you can eat and what not to), and in context of the overall prognosis and what you need to do logistically to make the patient's preferred choice happen. You then have a day or so to refine or add further questions or clarifications, as needed. It all sounds very obvious but it is a difficult topic, more often than not requiring the comparison of 'apples with pears', where there is rarely a black-and-white answer and emotions are running high. Some preparation is important. Also, be aware that there can be a lot of false summits; so be prepared for inconclusive oncological answers and advice. That is normal.

In the appointment with the consultant, a cancer patient may find it hard to ask certain questions. While you need to take your lead from the patient, it may be up to you to ensure the questions you have previously prepared with them get asked. I only attended a few consultant's appointments, but my role was to make sure all questions from the list were asked or covered and all answers captured. Note down everything said, like a stenographer, and do not forget to listen to the answer too. To use a rugby analogy, it is crucial that you are the fullback in the team: your job is to capture everything, and make sure absolutely nothing gets past you.

It may seem equally obvious but, just to emphasise, do not rely on your memory for the answers to your questions – take notes. It will be little surprise that conversations rarely follow the same course as a list of pre-prepared questions; so do not just make a list – leave gaps in the list to jot down notes. Consultants are usually flexible and generous with their time, but even so, I did have to do a 'quick-fire' round up of any remaining questions if time was tight. Then my furious scribbling might only pick up key words – BRCA negative, carboplatin, caelyx, paclitaxel, and so on. Even key words make a huge difference in helping to capture answers, especially when you are under time pressure. As soon as you have left the appointment, it is virtually certain that something will crop up. The patient may seek some reassuring clarification, and sometimes desperately need it. If you can authoritatively repeat word for word what the consultant has said, that can make a huge difference. Later I would tidy up my notes and share them, typed up, with Mum and Dad.

6.3.5 Other things you can do

Learn more. I privately spent some time trying to learn a bit more about her particular cancers – I wanted to understand more about the foe my mother was facing. Do not forget it is usually all new to the patient too. I reasoned that the more knowledge I could acquire, even basic knowledge, the more chance I had of understanding the oncologist's position, and I would be better informed as a sounding board. In any case, more knowledgeable heads (even if just about the basics) are most certainly better than fewer. So do some reading around – we all know we should take the internet with a bucket of salt, so consult with your oncologist, doctor, Macmillan nurse or other reliable sources. As well as being able to talk about it with my mum I wanted to be better informed so I could support my dad too. Finally, it also helped to field a few well-meant though sometimes misplaced or misjudged friendly suggestions from others.

Listen when talking things through with the cancer patient. I have always stuck steadfastly to talking about the facts and being diplomatically direct with Mum and Dad. You need to be a good listener too – and I do mean listen. You. Listen. To. Them. So many people do not actually listen but are too ready with their answers. Do not be one of those people: you will not add anything to the cancer sufferer's situation, and not listening can often make things worse. Do not be emotional or dismissive in your responses either, however well meant they may be. Mum found being told to 'think positive' really difficult. It highlights how someone has utterly failed to grasp the basics of what a cancer patient is facing. According to recent oncological research, 'think positive' isn't apparently yet a cure for cancer so do not say stuff like that. And unless you unfortunately also have terminal cancer or are otherwise subject to the certainty of an untimely death, no, you do not know what it is like.

Be open and honest as a sounding board. Did I try to be constructive? Sure, but based on the facts of the particular time. What was our next best step? Which weapons were left in our arsenal? I also noticed Mum liked to just be able to talk about the things that were happening, to discuss them – in particular, to be able to talk through the bad news. I have, on occasion, been told I am quite functional in how I approach things generally – in some difficult discussions, that default setting absolutely saved me from cracking. She just wanted to talk about it, talk it through – no judgment, no 'What about this?' or 'What about that?' If there had been bad news, it was important to acknowledge it head on. I always acknowledged the bad news but then immediately shifted focus on to which options were now on the table, however few they were. I know that sounds like trying to 'manage' the situation, but there is something about trying to focus on what the next best step is that supports the illusion of an element of control. It feels as if you have 'a plan', even if it just confirms the then current approach. However tenuous any semblance of a plan may be, it feels better to a cancer patient than seeming not to have a plan at all. Furthermore, for some cancer sufferers, hope becomes the only thing and relentlessly, dogmatically, always focusing on what could, and then can, be done was the only way I knew how to keep her hope alive.

Never give up. In the early days of Mum's diagnosis, before her options started to close down, it was easy to point to the fact of there being additional options. But over time, as options faded away one by one, conversation got more difficult. Your plan travels along an invisible continuum from proactive to reactive. And that is a problem. In a painfully slow and inescapable way, the basis for hope crumbles to dust. I cannot imagine what that does to someone psychologically. But then life decided it still had a card to play – when Mum's final option failed, almost as an afterthought, there was a less effective treatment, which was something better than nothing. However, as it turned out, the 'less effective' treatment was better and more effective than her previous 'better' treatment. For a while. We had another Christmas. That was wonderful.

It is all about them. Always defer to, and try to see things from the patient's perspective; otherwise, there is simply no point. No matter what your personal view is or how well-meaning you may be, suggest, do not impose, because it is always solely the patient's choice that counts. And that includes if they want to stop their treatment. This is about them – not you.

Be there for them. This was an area of personal growth for me. I easily fell into the stereotype of 'Men are from Mars'. There is nothing better for me than to see a problem and then provide a solution. Isn't providing a solution the whole point? I knew I could not cure Mum's cancer, so it was not that kind of solution, but more that I tended to think of things in a functional way: sorting out jobs, making a list of questions, running through notes, providing logistics or buying stuff. For example, because Mum could not move in her bed unaided, I bought an Alexa, so she could listen to music, radio or have an audiobook read to her at her command, instead of being in a hospice room barren of sound or companionship. Surely that was the best I could do? Well, no – not really. Listening and holding Mum's hand was. Being myself was. I recommend you do that too. Sometimes I'd recall memories to relive with her (as much to distract her as to remind her of happier times), read a book to her or just sit quietly beside her. Above all I just tried to be and act in the same normal way that she always knew me to be. That is all she wanted; and that is what someone may want of you too.

And another thing – remember when you were ill? What provided you with greater reassurance: a sad face looking at you, crying or bawling their eyes out, all full of emotion, or, someone sitting with you, talking calmly, listening and being composed? The latter is of much greater value – so watch yourself when you are in the room with the cancer sufferer. This is not about sugar-coating or trying to be happy, but it is about not carrying extra emotion or upset into the room for them to deal with; there will already be far too much of that. If you are feeling upset, do not visit; deal with it. Get yourself into a better place, and then visit. It is really very simple. In my head I would utterly scream at myself to 'man the **** up', followed by a mental narrative for a good few minutes, which was overwhelmingly expletive-ridden. At volume. But I could not go in upset – it was not good for Mum to see that. So get yourself in order. But one word of caution: if you bottle it up, do not forget to give yourself some 'you' time later – this is where your own support network comes in. This is important – be authentic and vulnerable with them. If, like me, that does not come easily to you, I cannot emphasise enough how critical it is to share how you are doing with your core support network. You need to share. You need to let your feelings out too.

6.3.6 The hospice

At some point after the diagnosis, you are pulled into the world of having to manage the disease. What you might be sold is the notion of managing the sufferer's oncological condition. It can be easy to buy that view – and why not? So, OK, there is no cure; but if we are careful, this can be managed. And if you manage the situation, the blackness of the fact that it is incurable is a slightly lighter shade of dark. But there are two problems with that: first, the cancer did not agree to being managed, and second, all too often, an oncological patient slips down the 'managing it' slope. Although you are aware there may be slippage, it is important not to miss how far the slippage has gone. The cancer patient will not. And then all too soon you realise your loved one is plainly out of options or just running on fumes. I cannot describe what witnessing that feels like – God only knows what it must be like to experience it.

It seems Mum's options are getting thin on the ground – you know this is the direction of travel but it still all seems so very fast and we wonder how the hell we got here so soon.

As I write, my mother has been in a hospice for a week. I suspect she thinks she may not come out. It is not an easy thing to review and clarify the order of service with her for her funeral, talk about her wishes and preferred place to pass, as well as other administrative matters including ensuring this, her journal, is published. What an unreal mundanity. I hope you never have to experience that with anyone you love; but if you do, above everything else I have written, you must be strong enough for both of you. I cannot stress this part enough. As her 'vitals' all gradually became critical it was the only time I lied to her. Hide the fact that you feel like you are being physically ripped apart inside. Lie through your teeth that you are OK. Fight the floods of tears you have privately. And be very convincing, every single time.

No. Matter. What.

You feel powerless. Helpless. I have seen her gaze a thousand-yard stare. I have sat beside her, desperately screaming as loud as I could in my head to come up with something to distract her. The best I can hope for is a fleeting distraction. In that moment, for a fraction of a second, she can be distracted. Maybe a momentary smile. But I know the next moment she is back in there, back facing her mental fight against the certainty of her outcome.

There is nothing she can do to stop her continued journey and she knows it. There is nothing anyone can do to stop the progression and we know it.

You look for the slightest glimmer of hope.

There is only one thing I can do – give my time and my love for whatever time she has left, whether that is more or less than consultants suggest. Be the family she wants around her – her only wish. I just want to show Mum the love she showed me every single day ever since I was born. Visiting the hospice and telling her that I love her is the most precious thing in the world, and I know my mum will take comfort from that. Also, do not underestimate the full-on power of a hug – she says she draws strength from a hug and thinks it is for her. Little does she know it is really for me.

6.3.7 Darkness

Mum passed away peacefully in mid-December 2020.

I cannot share what it feels like. I do not know the words. I just do not.

A month later.

There was a sense of the completion of the circle of life – the hospice had been built on the site of an old farm that had previously been a ruin for years. The farm was less than 100 metres from where Mum had grown up as a child – she had played in the old farm buildings with her sister and friends, in the very grounds that her room window looked out over. Home had always been important to her.

6.3.8 After the darkness – practical steps

The hospice had a leaflet providing guidance as to what happens after the death of a patient – concise practical steps for what needed to be done, who to contact and how. This was extremely useful; so ask your local hospice if they have something similar.

You will need to register the death with the governmental register of deaths – they do have a 'notify once' route in the UK (so all government departments such as HMRC, DVLA and so on that need to be aware are informed). That is the idea, but it does not always go exactly to plan, and we found that sometimes we had to notify them and then clarify that we had already notified them. But generally, it seemed to be OK.

Google will know the local funeral directors – funeral directors can help organise things including any local notices, as they know what needs to be done and how to do it. In the immediate aftermath of suffering such a big loss, getting to grips with, and doing what needs to be done may not be something you want to do. Others may want something to keep them busy. Each to their own, but my family was grateful for their help.

Even if you are not organising the funeral, you do still need to finalise or approve it: the funeral order of service, including hymns/prayers/music, burial or cremation with the priest or person leading the ceremony, inviting family and friends, and organising flowers or saying 'immediate family flowers only' in favour of donations and naming the charity or charities if that is what is preferred. If people are travelling, they may well need directions, potentially overnight accommodation – I sent a standard WhatsApp message to everyone. Additionally, we had Covid-19 restrictions to consider.

To focus on a few details . . . Where are they going to be buried? Was there a burial plan in place or had they already reserved a plot? If a cremation is chosen, will their ashes be kept or scattered? Depending on where the ashes are to be scattered, you may need to get permission from the landowner or relevant authorities – there are laws and regulations to be aware of. That is another benefit of using a funeral director – they will be able to give you advice on what you can and cannot do, as well as help organise a scattering ceremony, if you want one.

Consider whether there was a will – if so, you may wish to consult that, because, as well as providing for the distribution of the estate and possessions of someone who has passed away, it can also detail preferences about burial or cremation (and if it is a cremation, where they would like the ashes to be scattered). If they wanted a burial in a churchyard or cemetery, there are firm rules about the size and type of headstone or any memorial plaque – watch out for that, so consult the relevant religious minister. Also, getting a headstone may take several months; so be patient.

6.3.9 The funeral

Nearly six decades ago, my parents were married in the same church in which the funeral took place. It was almost Christmas in December 2020 and we were in lockdown for Covid-19; so the congregation was limited to 30 – and that had to include the priest and organist.

A slow drive-by was organised in a local car park for friends to have the opportunity to pay their last respects at 11 a.m. – we asked for people to be there for 10.55 a.m.; at 10.30 it started to rain. And it poured. How appropriate.

Driving around that car park, seeing people in ones and twos, and a lot of umbrellas out, I recognised one man, standing ramrod straight, staring ahead, with almost a military bearing. But what really got to me was that, while he clearly had made an effort to be as smart as possible, he was standing in the heavy rain without any umbrella, seemingly oblivious to the rain – as though he were defying it. He must have been soaked, but that was not going to stop him. He was standing proud, and looking straight ahead, unwaveringly. That brought a lump to my throat. I found that very hard. If we had circled for a second time through the car park, I know I would probably have cracked.

6.3.10 After the funeral

What a huge adjustment a surviving spouse has to make after a funeral.

At a time in life when routine may perhaps be more the order of the day than new things, life throws in one of its biggest and most stressful changes. That has got to be hard, not least after the funeral is over: people have left and the spouse is left at home, alone, where everything is a constant reminder. The last time my father ate a particular food, saw a particular TV programme, sat in a particular chair or commented on the garden, had been with Mum. And now there was a deafening silence. I did not feel I had to fill silences and you shouldn't too; sharing that moment is more important than what is said. I am sure it goes without saying there will be upset, and long pauses; occasionally, Dad just wanted to be on his own.

If you can, offer to stay with your surviving parent. I know that may not always be possible, and they may say they do not want to be a burden. But if you can spare some time, half a week or a week, in the immediate aftermath, and especially after the funeral, when everyone has gone home, I think they would overwhelmingly appreciate it. I was able to be around because of Covid-19 and being in my father's 'bubble'. I know Dad appreciated having someone else around.

I also engaged with my parents' friends, and made sure I obtained their contact details; I would recommend you do the same – especially if you, like me, are not local. Some people also pro-actively say they will check in. That is awesome – accept all the help you need. I also got the contact details of the cleaner, the fortnightly gardener, the butcher, the little local supplier of home-grown vegetables, and the on-line account details for the national supermarket website so I could remotely support Dad if needed. I got to know what my father typically ordered and, just as importantly, what he did not want to order. This marked my transition to focusing on supporting my father as the surviving spouse – you may not need most of these contact details; but if you do, it makes a huge difference to have them at your fingertips.

If you have been supporting someone being cared for at home, then any hospital equipment (bed, syringe driver, commode, and so on) and unused drugs need to be returned. Just contact your doctor or the hospital or hospice where the patient was, and they will usually organise a time to collect the items.

Other people need to be told of a cancer patient passing away. For the spouse, the reminders just keep coming – banks, credit card companies, loyalty card providers, utility companies, pension companies, insurance providers, the mobile phone company, doctors, opticians, the dentist and so on. Bank accounts may either need to be closed or changed from a joint account to a single account. They all have to be told. Having to have the same explanatory conversation over and over of 'my wife has died' must be almost unbearable. I came down one morning and saw a small pile of post, newsletters and circulars all addressed to Mum. Dad had marked them all as 'Return to sender, recipient deceased'. That stopped me in my tracks. There will be a lot to deal with, so pace yourself.

And then there are the clothes, shoes, handbags, keepsakes, jewellery and other personal effects. There can be some incredible and unique reminders. Support the surviving spouse, not just in their decision-making, but also, and equally importantly, in the speed of decision-making – they may not want to make an immediate decision. So far, my father has not chosen to go through Mum's belongings and 'sort them out'. Still having the personal items may feel a more tangible link to the person they have lost. He is starting to open up though – suggestions have included getting one of Mum's closest friends around to help go through all those reminders of Mum. It is a good suggestion but it is important to support him at his own pace.

The reality I found was that there is only so much you can do

– I needed to be conscious of when the support I was providing verged on organising my father, and that may be my not listening to what he wants or needs, or going at his pace. And that is all too easy to do. So I have stepped back and, although it sounds trite, I just make sure he has eaten properly. Exercise is important too; even if it is just walking. Also some level of social interaction is crucial; but again, this is at his pace. Ordinarily I like to crack on with an answer or solution; but I need to have patience, and allow my father time to adjust to his revised new world, reality and regime, and trust that, if he needs me, he will say so. That will not stop my looking out for my father, as I am sure it would not stop you; but you and I have to let them be in charge.

My plan was just to be there for my father for the immediate aftermath, during Christmas 2020 and into the New Year. But as I write this the country is in lockdown with Covid-19 and has been for several months now. Given that I am working from home, it is easy to stay with him and I know it is good for him too. That said, I do feel the need to get back to my flat, my home and my routine. I also need to do it for 'me'. I have mentioned a few times the need to look after yourself when you are providing support and to have your own support network. Now I need some time to rebalance, some space and time alone, and I need to do that in my own home. Mum's illness spanned six years and I have to pace myself to support my father. But no matter what, I will be here for him too – and going away is the only way I can come back.

6.3.11 Do not forget about you

You have lost someone too.

And you do not always know how you may react.

I could not be bothered with work, something I am not well known for. It just seemed utterly pointless. I felt hollow. Directionless. Empty. Nothing seemed to matter.

Things can blindside you too. I needed to make a grocery shopping list for my father last week, and reached for a pad of paper, opening it to find the next free page. There, I found a page with a shopping list already handwritten. By Mum.

Prioritise caring for how you are feeling too. Be authentic with others as well as yourself. Allow yourself time to grieve – do not let the fact that you are supporting a remaining loved one obscure or occlude the fact that you have lost someone who meant so much to you too.

Use your support network. This seems to be a recurring theme, but it does underscore precisely how important it is. I know that I am extremely lucky: I have some great friends, without whom my journey would have been a lot harder – there are no two ways about it.

You may find yourself on a journey too. Allow yourself to go on that journey, and to grieve. Accept that you need to process what has happened to you, the emotional pressure and strain that you have been under, and ultimately, give yourself permission to grieve. It is a natural process, and part of being a human being; so be kind to yourself. As for my journey, I know I will confidently carry Mum with me for the rest of my life. I will celebrate her life, not mourn it – that is not to say I will not crushingly miss her every single day. I know I will, it is just that I will not mourn. Instead, I will be for ever grateful for the time I shared with her. The best way I can put it to you is this: there have been hundreds of millions of people who have lived, billions currently living, and who knows how many trillions yet to live. So genuinely, what are the odds I would be born in the same century or country as this woman, or that I would ever meet her? Yet not only did I know her, but she was my mum and close friend. And that has got to be a wonderful thing. I will treasure that thought and, because of it, wherever I am, I know that she will be there because I will always take her with me.

PART 6: INVOLVING OTHER PEOPLE

Annex – some cancer organisations and their contact details

(The individual websites will be able to direct you to your local resources where these are available)

Cancer Charity	Address	Website
British Gynaecological Cancer Society	C/O William Denton CYF, Bangor, LL57 4FE administrator@bgcs.org.uk	https://www.bgcs.org.uk
Breast Cancer Now	Breast Cancer Now Ibex House 42-47 Minories London EC3N 1DY Tel: 03332070300 hello@breastcancernow.org	https://breastcancernow.org
Cancer Research UK	Cancer Research UK PO BOX 1561 Oxford OX4 9GZ Tel: 0300 123 4452 Nurse Helpline 0808 800 4040	https://www.cancerresearchuk.org
Cochrane Breast Cancer	Cochrane Breast Cancer 11-13 Cavendish Square London, W1G 0AN United Kingdom Tel: +44 207 183 7503	https://breastcancer.cochrane.org
Eve Appeal, (The)	The Eve Appeal 10-18 Union Street London SE1 1SZ	office@eveappeal.org.uk
Go Girls - supporting your cancer Journey	44 The Ridgeway, Upwey, Dorset DT3 5QQ Tel: +441305 255719	https://www.gogirlssupport.org
Guy's Cancer Charity	Cancer Centre at Guy's Great Maze Pond, London SE1 9RT Tel: 020 7188 7188, extension 56805	https://guyscancercharity.org.uk

Cancer Charity	Address	Website
Jo's Cervical Cancer Trust	Jo's Cervical Cancer Trust, 10-18 Union St, London SE1 1SZ Tel: 0808 802 8000 info@jostrust.org.uk	https://www.jostrust.org.uk/
Macmillan Cancer Support	Macmillan Cancer Support (head Office) 89 Albert Embankment London, SE1 7UQ Macmillan Support Line Tel: 080 880 80000	https://www.macmillan.org.uk
Maggie's	Maggie's 20 St. James Street London W6 9RW (See their website for Maggie's more local to you) Tel: 0300 123 1801	https://www.maggies.org
Marie Curie	Marie Curie One Embassy Gardens 8 Viaduct Gardens London SW11 7BW Support Line Tel: 0800 090 2309	https://www.mariecurie.org.uk/
The Royal Marsden Hospital	The Royal Marsden Hospital (London) royalmarsden.nhs.uk Fulham Road, London SW3 6JJ Tel: 020 7352 8171	https://www.royalmarsden.nhs.uk

Cancer Magazines	Description	Website
C3 Magazine	The Clatterbridge Cancer C3 magazine for staff, members and patients of The Clatterbridge Cancer Centre in Liverpool, the Wirral and Merseyside. They host the only UK facility providing low-energy proton beam therapy for rare eye cancer treatment	https://www.clatterbridgecc.nhs.uk/patients/general-information/c3-magazine
Vita	The Breast Cancer magazine with articles about health and	https://breastcancernow.org/information-support/publication/vita-current-issue

	wellbeing for people living with or beyond, breast cancer	
Cancerworld Magazine	Cancerworld is an online magazine and website for oncologists, other cancer professionals, policy makers and also patient advocates	https://cancerworld.net
Macmillan Inside Information	'Inside Information' is a quarterly email summary of new information resources. It is for Macmillan professionals but also anyone interested in Macmillan-based cancer information	cancerinformationteam@macmillan.org.uk
Ovacome	Ovacome is a membership charity for those suffering with ovarian cancer. It is free to join. Members have a free magazine 3 times a year Tel: 0800 008 7054/07503 682 311	https://www.ovacome.org.uk
Action Magazine (Ovarian Cancer Action)	Online magazine about improving ovarian cancer survival rates	https://ovarian.org.uk/action-mag

Other Country Cancer Charities	**Address**	**Website**
Australia		
Cancer Australia	Locked Bag 3, Strawberry Hills NSW 2012 Tel: Free call 1800 624 973	https://www.canceraustralia.gov.au/impacted-cancer/cancer-support-organisations
Canada		
The Canadian Cancer Society	Canadian Cancer Society 55 St. Clair Avenue West, Suite 300 Toronto, ON M4V 2Y7, Canada Tel free: 1-888-939-3333	https://cancer.ca
India		
Indian Cancer Society	National Head Quarters 74, Jerbai Wadia Road, Bhoiwada, Parel, Mumbai - 400012 (India) Tel: +91- 22-2413 9445 / 51 info@indiancancersociety.org	https://www.indiancancersociety.org

Ireland

Irish Cancer Society	43/45 Northumberland Road Dublin, D04 VX65 Tel: +353-1-231-0500 info@irishcancersociety.ie	https://www.cancer.ie/

New Zealand

The Cancer Society New Zealand	The Cancer Society national Office PO Box 651, Wellington 6140 Tel: 0800 226 237	https://www.cancer.org.nz

Northern Ireland

Cancer Focus Northern Ireland	40-44 Eglantine Avenue Belfast BT9 6DX Northern Ireland Tel: 028 9066 3281 hello@cancerfocusni.org Cancer information and support Nurseline is available Monday – Friday 9am to 1pm. Tel: 0800 783 3339 Email our nurses: nurseline@cancerfocusni.org	https://cancerfocusni.org/
Northern Ireland Cancer Network	1st Floor, SPPG (DoH), 12-22 Linenhall Street, Belfast BT2 8BS Tel: 02895 363305 nican.office@hscni.net	https://nican.hscni.net/

Scotland

Cancer Support Scotland	Calman Centre, 75 Shelley Road, Gartnavel Campus, Glasgow, G12 0ZE Tel: 0800 652 4531 Email: info@cancersupportscotland.org	https://www.cancersupportscotland.org/

South Africa

The Cancer Association of South Africa	National Head Office 26 Concorde Road West, Bedfordview, 2008, Johannesburg, Gauteng Tel: 011-616 7662 Email: info@cansa.org.za	https://cansa.org.za

USA

American Cancer Society - Cancer Action Network	655 15th Street, NW, Suite 503 Washington, DC 20005 Tel: +1 (202) 661-5700	https://www.fightcancer.org/

Wales

Cancer Research Wales	22 Neptune Court, Vanguard Way, Cardiff, CF24 5PJ Tel: +44 29 2185 5050 us@cancerresearchwales.org.uk	https://www.cancerresearch.wales/

Index

A&E [Accident and Emergency]	27
Anger	48, 46, 47, 107
Blood tests	42, 60
Bowel problems	41
BRCA [gene]	116
Caelyx [(liposomal Adriamycin) a chemotherapy drug for breast cancer]	116
Cancer: Breast	18, 24, 60
Cancer diagnosis	45, 48, 60, 61, 67, 92, 105, 106
Cancer marker test	114
Cancer Ovarian	31, 52, 60
Cancer patient [the]	106, 111, 112, 118, 122
Cancer [return of; recurrence]	59, 61
Cancer sufferer	55, 80, 104, 118, 119, 121
Cancer terminal	118
Carboplatin [chemotherapy drug to treat ovarian and lung cancer]	116
Chemotherapy	23, 40, 41, 43, 53, 56, 66, 68, 69, 72, 96, 97,
Consultant's appointments [preparation]	115, 116,
Daydreaming	86, 87
Despair	30
Disbelief	47, 107
DVLA [to contact post a death]	126
'Facetime' [the value of]	112
Fear	12, 14, 19, 20, 25, 27, 30, 31, 36, 40, 41, 46, 47, 59, 61, 106
Hair loss	42, 115
HMRC	126
Hospice	13-15, 46, 65, 73, 78, 79, 80, 111, 121-125, 130
Hospital Chaplaincy teams	83

Lists of questions [Consultants
appointments; as a way to support] 115 - 117, 120

Macmillan 21, 22, 24, 46, 51, 52,
  55, 56, 58, 78-80, 117
Maggie's Centre 45
Medical students 28, 92

Nausea 41, 52, 57
NED (no evidence of disease) 41
Neighbours 76
Network [of support] 109-114, 122, 130, 133
NHS 12, 21, 32, 33, 45, 52, 56, 77, 98

Oncologists 92
Oncology Health Service / Department 45, 46

Paclitaxel [chemo drug] 42, 116
Palliative Care team 96
Palliative Counsellor 46, 80
Pixie hair [result of chemo] 42
Powerless [being] 106, 123

Radiotherapy 23, 24, 28, 29, 33, 43
Reflection [time for] 44, 49, 50, 54, 80
The Royal Marsden [(sic) Hospital] 55, 56

Sleep 29-31, 33, 34,
Social Services 77, 78
Strategy [is important to have] 51, 53, 62, 76

Take notes 116

University 3, 15, 65

Way for people to help 78
Will(s) 78, 79, 127

Printed in Great Britain
by Amazon